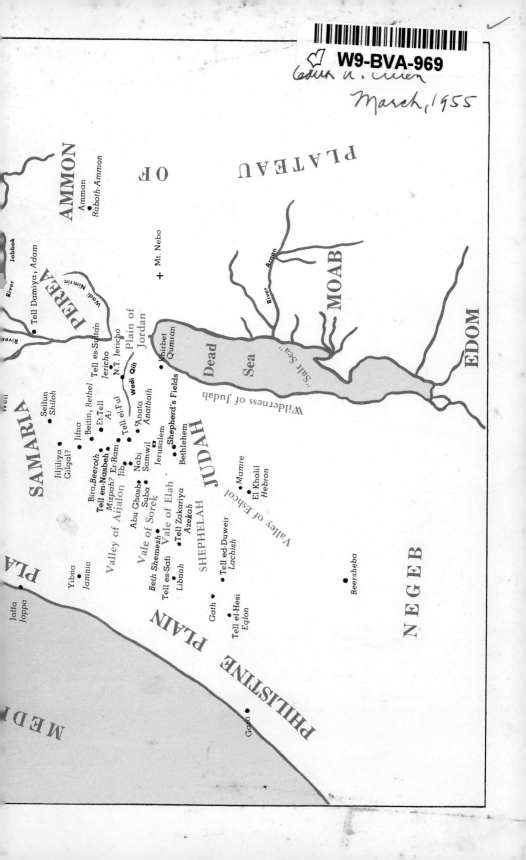

Edith N. Allen

March, 1955

Cradle of Our Faith

The Dome of the Rock — site of Solomon's Temple in Jerusalem — a symbol of three great faiths: Judaism, Christianity and Islam (see page 61).

Cradle of Our Faith

The Holy Land

JOHN C. TREVER

A. J. Humphreys Professor of Religion
Morris Harvey College

PHOTOGRAPHS BY THE AUTHOR
SKETCHES BY D-EON PRIEST

UNITED STATES JUNIOR CHAMBER OF COMMERCE

1954

Library of Congress Catalogue Card Number: 54-12621

Second Printing December, 1954

TYPOGRAPHY BY CARL HERTZOG

Printed in the United States of America
Newsfoto Publishing Company
San Angelo, Texas

PREFACE

INSPIRED by the words of their Creed, "We believe that faith in God gives meaning and purpose to human life," the United States Junior Chamber of Commerce, with the support of their Religious Activities Committee, resolved to develop a project through which these words might be emphasized. This resolve, strengthened by the Committee's visit to the large topographical reconstruction of the Holy Land at Chautauqua, New York, became the vision of this book.

Among the great religions of the world, three — Judaism, Christianity, and Islam — look to Palestine as a sacred heritage of their faith. That little country, barely 150 miles in length by sixty miles at its widest point, is the Holy Land to nearly a billion people. Almost as sharply divided as the geographical features of that small country are the people who recognize it as the Holy Land of their faith. Although widely different in their customs of worship and theological points of view — even within these three faiths as well as between them — there is a bond of unity in the Holy Land, the cradle of the faith of each. There is unity in the fact of faith in God and in the common heritage of many persons through whom God has spoken. There is unity in historic events, places and geographical features of the country. There is unity in Scriptures recognized as the Word of God: the Old Testament of Jews, the New Testament of Christians, the Koran of Muslims.

There is one further point of unity within these faiths which is intensely relevant for our times — their common teaching of the brotherhood of man. With the hope that through a better understanding of these points of unity within and between these faiths, a closer fellowship might be obtained, the Junior Chamber of Commerce has launched this book for all. May the simple telling of the facts underlying this common heritage in the Holy Land, together with natural color photographs from the country, awaken within all who study this book a response of faith in God and an awareness of those abiding ties which draw mankind closer together.

The author wishes to express his sincere appreciation to the many who have generously given of their time and counsel in order to help this book achieve its purpose. Especially is he indebted to the American Schools of Oriental Research (which granted the author a fellowship for study in the Holy Land in 1947-1948); Rabbi Harold Friedman, Temple Hesed Abraham, Jamestown, New York; the Reverend Carl F. Zietlow, Director for Development, Northeastern Division, National Conference of Christians and Jews; Dr. Max Arzt, Vice Chancellor, Jewish Institute of Theological Studies; Dr. Moses Jung, Consultant in Catholic-Jewish Relations, American Jewish Committee, and Chairman, Columbia University Seminar on Inter-religious Relations; the Reverend Dr. Louis F. Hartman, Executive Secretary, Catholic Biblical Association of America; Imam Khalil Ahmad Nasir, the American Fazl Mosque, Washington, D.C.; Dr. W. F. Albright, W. W. Spence Professor of Semitic Languages, Johns Hopkins University; Dr. Millar Burrows, Winkley Professor of Biblical Theology, Yale University Divinity School; Mr. Harry G. Wiles, Treasurer, Junior Chamber International; Mr. Ralph C. Allmon, and Mr. F. M. Warburton, J. C. I. Senators; my colleagues, Dr. R. L. Lasley, Professor of English, and Dean Ashby C. Blackwell; and my patient and ever-helpful wife.

JOHN C. TREVER

Charleston, West Virginia
March, 1954

Foreword

The statements on the following four pages were
written especially for this book by representatives
of the faiths that look to the Holy Land for their
spiritual heritage. These are presented in the
order of the historical appearance of each faith.

JUDAISM

CATHOLIC CHRISTIANITY

ISLAM

PROTESTANT CHRISTIANITY

What the Holy Land Means to

The Jewish Faith

THERE is hardly a site in the Holy Land that does not hold religious or historic meaning for the Jews. The ideals and the faith which saw their birth in this Holy Land have continued to inspire Jews everywhere with the hope that men of good will, in every faith, will recognize one another as brothers and thus bring peace to the whole world. It was here that the seeds of democracy first took root; the recognition of man as fellow man; the emphasis on human dignity; the possibility of self-determination. These principals were exemplified in the lives of the Patriarchs and in the immortal Mosaic commandments, "Love the LORD, thy God, with all thy heart, and all thy soul, and all thy might," and "Love thy neighbor as thyself."

It was David, the warrior-poet, King of Israel, to whom tradition has ascribed the composition of many of the Psalms, who established Jerusalem as his capital. In the hearts of the ancient Jewish people Jerusalem became a symbol of their life as well as their religion. As the prophets unfolded the implications of true monotheism, Jerusalem acquired universal significance and became the spiritual capital, "the perfection of beauty, the joy of all the earth."

All through the Middle Ages and into modern times, as Jews moved to the far corners of the earth, the Holy Land remained their spiritual ideal. For of Zion the prophet Isaiah proclaimed that many people would say:

> *"Come, let us go up to the mountain of the LORD,*
> *to the house of the God of Jacob;*
> *that he may teach us his ways*
> *and that we may walk in his paths."*
> *For out of Zion shall go forth the law,*
> *and the word of the LORD from Jerusalem. (2: 3)*

Sings the famous medieval poet, Judah Ha-Levi:

> *Would I were wandering in these places dear*
> *Where God revealed himself in ages past*
> *Showing his light to messenger and seer.*

DR. MOSES JUNG
Consultant in Catholic-Jewish Relations
American Jewish Committee

What the Holy Land Means to

The Catholic Faith

GOD guides the destinies of men and nations, from Adam to the end of the world. He led fallen man up from the primitive conditions of countless centuries into the first urban cultures of Mesopotamia and Egypt. He it was who chose the fair little country that lay between these two great centers of ancient civilization to be the land where He would reveal His will and develop His plan for man's salvation.

Here He taught the Patriarchs to walk before Him in Holiness. Here He spoke to the Prophets. Here He prepared His Chosen People to be the nucleus of His new, worldwide Israel. To this land He sent from heaven His own Son, born of the Virgin Mary, that in Him all men should find peace and happiness.

The Israel that is Catholic (which means "universal") soon outgrew the narrow confines of Palestine. But a grown man, even after he has traveled far and wide, does not forget his birthplace. Jerusalem still remains the cradle of Christianity. To this Holy City, and to every inch of this land that has been made sacred by the holy men and women of both Testaments who trod its soil, the Christian heart will ever turn in love and veneration.

THE REVEREND DR. LOUIS F. HARTMAN
Executive Secretary
Catholic Biblical Association of America
Catholic University of America
Washington, D. C.

What the Holy Land Means to

The Muslim Faith

THE Muslim veneration of the Holy Land is many-fold in nature. Islam teaches acceptance of and belief in all Prophets of God. The Muslims call Abraham "The Father of Prophets." The Prophet Muhammad was an Ishmaelite, a descendant of Abraham. Thus the Muslim tradition is connected with the Holy Land from very early times.

For a Muslim all the Prophets of the Holy Land (particularly Abraham, Moses and Jesus) are a part of his spiritual heritage. "We make no distinction between any of His Messengers," says the Holy Koran (2: 285), the Holy Scripture of Islam.

In the Holy Koran, the words "Glory be to Him Who carried His servant from the Sacred Mosque to the Distant Mosque the environs of which We have blessed" refer to a very significant vision of the Prophet Muhammad. In this spiritual experience, the Holy Prophet was carried from Mecca to Jerusalem. Before God commanded the Prophet to face toward the Ka'aba (in Mecca) during his prayers, he offered his prayers facing toward Jerusalem.

For the last thirteen centuries the Holy Land has been considered by the Muslims as one of their most important spiritual centers. The reverence given to this land has been second only to Mecca and Medina. Nothing will in any way dim the glory and luster of this venerated Land from the hearts of four hundred million Muslims of the world.

MR. KHALIL AHMAD NASIR
Imam (Minister) of the
  American Fazl Mosque
Washington, D. C.

What the Holy Land Means to

The Protestant Faith

THE Holy Land is the great paradox of historical geography. Here is a tiny land, considered poor in natural resources — yet it has become the geographical parent of Judaism and Christianity, and the progenitor of Islam. In antiquity it played scarcely any political part, yet it nurtured the most powerful spiritual forces of history. Smallest of the subdivisions of the Roman Empire, it set in motion a faith that was to conquer the Empire and to enthrone Christ in the capital of Caesar. In the Middle Ages this little country was to become a symbol of faith, locking East and West in a contest which deeply affected all subsequent history.

What has made the Holy Land such a focus of history? It was for one thing the bridge between different parts of the oldest complex of our ancestral civilization. All movement of culture between such centers as Egypt and Mesopotamia passed over it. Its geographical character prevents it from becoming the base of empire, and effectively discourages the accumulation of wealth. The perpetual uncertainty of rainfall forbids excessive reliance on material goods, forcing men to found their hopes on the unseen. Terrain and climate encourage the believer to emulate the prophets of old, who sought to commune with their God in solitude within a few miles of ancient cities.

But beyond all environmental factors lies a great miracle of history, a lasting monument to the vitality of Faith.

DR. WILLIAM F. ALBRIGHT
*W. W. Spence Professor of
Semitic Languages
Johns Hopkins University
Baltimore, Maryland*

CREED

of the
UNITED STATES JUNIOR CHAMBER OF COMMERCE

WE BELIEVE:

That faith in God gives

        meaning and purpose to human life;

That the brotherhood of man transcends

        the sovereignty of nations;

That economic justice can best be won

        by free men through free enterprise;

That government should be of laws

        rather than of men;

That earth's great treasure

        lies in human personality;

And that service to humanity

        is the best work of life.

CONTENTS

Contents continued

SUPPLEMENTS

INDICES

Cradle of Our Faith

Note: The spelling of Arabic place-names follows that of the 1:250,000 maps prepared by the Survey of Palestine, 1946.

Since most of the photographs were taken in 1947 and 1948, some changes in modern buildings have occurred and may be noticed by recent visitors to the Holy Land.

Introducing the Holy Land

L YING astride the crossroads of the Middle East, the Holy Land has for more than three thousand years borne the clash of political forces and destructive armies bringing devastation to her cities and tragedy to her people. Despite the struggles that have raged for control of this country, values far more important for the world than kingdoms, power and material possessions have emerged from her tumultuous history. The ideals of faith, love, devotion and submission to the will of God, the Father of us all, are the lessons this land has taught — the symbols for which she stands.

To this land, then, we go to learn of her ancient past; to study the remains of cities and cultures of long ago; to see her mountains, valleys, lakes, rivers and plains; but above all to absorb the lessons of life she would have us learn.

Although but a small country, the Holy Land is as peculiarly varied in geography and climate as any part of the globe. Along the coast of the Mediterranean lies a plain, varying in width from a few hundred yards to more than fifteen miles. Rising steeply to the east of this plain is a ridge of mountains. They reach their greatest height[1] northwest of the Sea of Galilee.[2] The Galilean ridge is cut off from the ridge to the south by the broad plain of Esdraelon[3] which runs from the coast to the Jordan Valley.

The mountains of Samaria, beginning at Mount Gilboa,[4] and the Judean highlands continue the central ridge until it slopes off gradually into the Negeb south of Hebron and Beersheba. East of the highlands is the Great Rift in which lie the Sea of Galilee,[5] the Jordan Valley, and the Dead Sea.[6] The high plateau of Transjordan ascends sharply east of the Jordan and merges finally into the blistering desert of Arabia.

At the focal point of this ancient and beloved land, and spreading out over two hills in the Judean highlands, is Jerusalem — the Holy City extolled in song and story. Scholars have disputed the origin of the name, but it has often been interpreted to mean "vision of peace"[7] or "possession of peace." Although anything but peaceful through its many centuries of turbulent history, Jerusalem has been the fountainhead of a spiritual power which has made it the Holy City to millions of people. It continues to be the symbol of their faith in God.

Countless pilgrims have stood breathless at the sight of its gates; many

---

[1] Mount Jarmaq, almost 4000 feet.
[2] See plate 24.
[3] Called "the 'Emeq" today. See plates 13c, 18b and 23b.
[4] See plate 13c.
[5] 685 feet below sea level.
[6] 1275 feet below sea level.
[7] Luke 19: 42.

Looking west from the Mount of Olives, across the Valley of the Kidron to the Old City of

[Plate 1]

have trod its streets in reverent awe, bending in silent prayer before its sacred shrines. No other city on earth arouses such emotions in so many.

Jerusalem, today spreading far to the north and west beyond its ancient boundaries, sits high on the "backbone" of the Holy Land.[1] Normally the Mediterranean Sea to the west sends cooling breezes to provide a healthful and temperate climate. Occasionally, however, torrid sirocco winds blow from the east, filling the air with fine sand, bringing discomfort and often fever. To the east Jerusalem is flanked by the deep Valley of the Kidron. Beyond is the Mount of Olives,[2] screening from view the barren wilderness[3] which continues some fifteen miles eastward to the Jordan Valley.[4]

In the view on the opposite page, we are standing on the side of the Mount of Olives, looking west across the Valley of the Kidron to what was in ancient times the northern extremity of the city where the Temple stood. Today the large domed building at the right in the photograph, called the Dome of the Rock, occupies that ancient site.[5] At the extreme left stands the Church of the Dormition, which dominates the western hill.

Just beyond the wall of the city extends the long, low rooftop of the Mosque el Aksa, the third most sacred mosque in the Muslim world. Above this rooftop appear the domes of the Tiphereth Yisrael and the Hurva synagogues, the two oldest Jewish synagogues in the Old City of Jerusalem.[6] Beyond the Dome of the Rock rise the towers of Christian churches and monasteries.

Here, then, is the city of many churches — the Holy City. Commercially unimportant and surrounded by little fertile soil, Jerusalem is still unique in history for its spiritual meaning. It is a center of worship, a symbol of our faith.

Back through the pages of history, therefore, let us go to watch the drama of the ancient past unfold the growth of that faith in God. The many centuries covered by the story permit, of course, the selection of only brief episodes.

Modern scenes in natural color have been chosen in order to portray as much of the Holy Land as possible. Thus the reader may become acquainted with many of the features of the land. The photographs can be only symbolic of that ancient story, since the onslaught of time has wrought many changes. Still the general features of the country remain unchanged, and many historic places have now been identified. In most cases the original sites are only hills, called *tells,* with evidences of early occupation beneath the surface. With a little imagination, however, many stories can come to life as we see the places where they occurred.

---

[1] About 2600 feet above sea level.
[2] See plate 26a.
[3] See plate 20a.
[4] See plate 8b.
[5] See *Frontispiece* and plates 15c, 30.
[6] Both destroyed in 1948.

a. A Bedouin encampment near modern Jifna in the hill country of Ephraim.

b. Mount Ebal beside site of Shechem, Abraham's first settlement in the land of Canaan.

[Plate 2]

Early Beginnings

(Gophna — Shechem)

¶ Now the LORD said to Abram, "Go from your country and your kindred and your father's house to the land that I will show you. . . ."[1] ¶ When they had come to the land of Canaan, Abram passed through the land to the place at Shechem, to the oak of Moreh.[2] ¶ By faith Abraham obeyed when he was called . . .[3]

THE great civilizations of Babylonia and Egypt had been flourishing for many centuries when the story of faith we seek to trace began — almost 3900 years ago. At that time the Aramean patriarch,[4] Abraham, was moved to leave his home in Haran, a small town far to the northeast of the Holy Land.

Archeologists have shown that there were many movements of peoples in the Middle East for several centuries after 2000 B.C. Some drifted out of the steppes of Arabia to the south and others moved up and down the fertile valleys, especially along the coastal lands on the west and in the Tigris-Euphrates Valley on the east.

The more stable civilization of Palestine during the previous centuries was declining. Nomadic and semi-nomadic wanderers pressed into its highland country with their flocks and herds. It is not possible to date precisely the movement of Abraham from his Aramean homeland into the "land of Canaan," but the description of his wanderings in Genesis 12 fits naturally into this period of ethnic movements.

The upper photograph shows a modern Bedouin (nomad) encampment with its black goat's-hair tents, beside Jifna[5] in the central highlands. Though such encampments are gradually disappearing from the Middle Eastern scene, they symbolize well the movements of the semi-nomadic Hebrew tribes of patriarchal times. This valley beside Jifna[6] witnessed some of the movements of the patriarchs. The olive trees on the far slope, important today in the economy of the country, resemble the wooded hills that probably greeted Abraham and his family long ago.

He stopped first at Shechem,[7] which lay between Mount Gerizim[8] and Mount Ebal several miles north of Jifna. The eastern edge of the modern village of Balata is visible in the lower photograph at the foot of Mount Ebal. Surrounded by sacred oak trees, the domed Tomb of Joseph appears in this scene at the extreme right.[9] Some remains of ancient Shechem have been uncovered just left of the area shown by the photograph.

Later Abraham moved farther south near Bethel,[10] about three miles southeast of Jifna, and then on to the Negeb, south of Beersheba.

---

[1] Genesis 12: 1.
[2] Genesis 12: 5b, 6a.
[3] Hebrews 11: 8a.
[4] Deuteronomy 26: 5.
[*] "c." stands for circa, meaning "about."
[5] Gophna of later Maccabean times.
[6] Perhaps ancient Ophni of Joshua 18: 24.
[7] Genesis 12: 6.
[8] See plate 4c.
[9] Joshua 24: 32.
[10] Genesis 12: 8.

a. Haram Ramet el-Khalil, the probable site of Abraham's encampment at Mamre.

b. Hebron from the northwest. Mosque at left stands over the tombs of the Hebrew Patriarchs.

[Plate 3]

Early Settlements

(MAMRE — HEBRON)

¶ *So Abram moved his tent, and came and dwelt by the oaks of Mamre, which are at Hebron; and there he built an altar to the* LORD.[1]

DURING a famine in the Holy Land Abraham moved on into Egypt.[2] On his return from there he established his camp at the "oaks (or terebinths) of Mamre" near Hebron, about twenty miles south of Jerusalem. In the region of Mamre, Hebron and the Negeb, the patriarchal encampments remained for a long time.

An old oak tree, called Abram's Oak, is shown to tourists today in the gardens of a Russian Orthodox monastery southwest of Hebron in the Valley of Eshcol. Excavators, however, have unearthed what is very probably the original site of Mamre two miles north of Hebron at Haram Ramet el-Khalil — "The Sanctuary of the Hill of the Friend" (upper photograph).

The large building foundation shows clearly the type of construction used by King Herod in the 1st century B.C., and other evidence points to its long history as a sacred site. Part of the modern name, *El-Khalil,* meaning "The Friend," clearly refers to Abraham,[3] who is revered by Jews, Christians and Muslims. No oaks are found there, for it is surrounded by fig orchards; but there is an old tradition that a sacred terebinth tree stood at one time on the site.

One of the most delightful stories of the Old Testament describes Abraham's purchase of the Cave of Machpelah[4] from the Hittites who lived nearby in Hebron. Here the patriarchs were buried, and there is little doubt that the ancient cave is correctly located under the great sacred area of the present Muslim mosque.

The southwest corner of the mosque with its tower—the minaret from which the *muezzin* calls the faithful Muslims to prayer — appears at the left in the lower picture, just beyond the veiled women. Here again, the massive construction of the 1st century B.C. can be seen in a beautiful state of preservation, topped by recent Arab architecture.

From Numbers 13: 22 it is apparent that Hebron was not built until about 1700 B.C., "seven years before Zoan in Egypt." It attained strategic importance in later Hebrew history. There the spies found the luscious fruit in the Valley of Eshcol during the Exodus.[5] The city was David's capital for seven years after the death of Saul.[6]

Sacred to Jews, Christians and Muslims, Hebron is today called *El-Khalil,* "The Friend," in memory of the shepherd Abraham who was a friend though a stranger in the land.[7]

---

[1] Genesis 13: 18.
[2] See plate 5 and page 11.
[3] Isaiah 41: 8.
[4] Genesis 23.
[5] Numbers 13.
[6] 2 Samuel 2: 1-3; 5: 1-5; see page 29.
[7] Genesis 23: 4.

a. The hills of Gilead with the Jabbok River Valley in the distance at the left.

b. Jacob's Well surrounded by a partly finished Greek Orthodox church.

c. Jacob's Well at the foot of Mount Gerizim, location of the Samaritan temple.

[Plate 4]

The Wanderings of Jacob

(River Jabbok — Jacob's Well)

¶ So Jacob called the name of the place Peniel, saying, "For I have seen God face to face, and yet my life is preserved."[1]

¶ And Jacob came safely to the city of Shechem . . . And . . . he bought for a hundred pieces of money the piece of land on which he had pitched his tent.[2]

THE story of the life of Jacob, grandson of Abraham, touches many places in the Holy Land, but we can visit only two. The well-known account of Jacob's wrestling with the stranger near the River Jabbok in the hill country of Gilead introduces the region "beyond the Jordan," usually referred to as Transjordan.

In the upper scene, the cultivated valley leads off to the Jabbok River Valley in the distance, not too far from the point where Jacob's struggle must have occurred at Peniel,[3] according to the story in Genesis 32: 22-32. Jacob's concern over meeting his brother Esau, whom he had tricked out of his birthright many years before, illustrates the struggle of his conscience over ethical principles which were emerging from his faith in God.

After his reconciliation with Esau, Jacob crossed the Jordan and settled at Shechem, where Abraham had first stopped. The center and lower photographs portray this historic site. Here Jacob purchased land from the native Canaanites in the rich plain (shown in the center photograph) east of Shechem. There he dug the well that still bears his name — one of the most certain of the ancient sites of the Holy Land. A partly finished Greek Orthodox church surrounds the ancient well and the garden of the monastery.

In the lower view, the walled monastery garden backs up toward the foot of famed Mount Gerizim. To the right of the monastery lies a narrow valley between Mount Gerizim and Mount Ebal,[4] at the mouth of which is the modern village of Balata (just out of this scene). It is now known to be the site of ancient Shechem and probably Sychar of the Gospel of John 4: 5.[5]

Beyond Mount Gerizim to the west is Nablus, where live remnants of the Samaritans. In the time of Nehemiah, many centuries after the life of Jacob, they opposed the Jews of Jerusalem who rejected them.[6] After the schism they built their own temple for worship on top of this mountain. The annual celebration by the Samaritans of the Feast of the Passover still is an event of great attraction for tourists. The small building, barely discernible on the crest of the mountain in the left-hand portion of the photograph, is a Muslim *weli* or sacred place, not the Samaritan temple.

---

[1] Genesis 32: 30.
[2] Genesis 33: 18-19.

[3] For later events centered here see Judges 8, 2 Samuel 18, 1 Kings 17: 1, and page 33.

[4] See plate 2b.
[5] See plate 25b and page 51.
[6] c. 450 B.C.; Nehemiah 4, 6.

[9]

a. The Sphinx and the great Pyramid of Khufu at Gizeh, southwest of Cairo, Egypt.

b. The Valley of the Tombs of the Kings seen from the Temple of Karnak at ancient Thebes.

[Plate 5]

Sojourn in Egypt

(Gizeh — Thebes)

¶ *Then Joseph settled his father [Jacob] and his brothers, and gave them a possession in the land of Egypt, in the best of the land, in the land of Rameses [Goshen], as Pharaoh had commanded.*[1]

FAMINE drove the Hebrew patriarch Jacob and his family into Egypt about 1700 B.C.[2] The familiar story of Joseph's rise to power in Egypt and the settlement of his brothers in the rich land of Goshen in the Nile Delta[3] falls logically into the era when Egypt was ruled by the Hyksos, aggressive Semitic rulers from Syria.

Seizing control of Egypt late in the 18th century B.C., the Hyksos established their capital at Zoan, later called Rameses. Apparently the Hebrews settled somewhat south in the rich valley extending from Lake Timsah, on the edge of Sinai, to the Nile.

Egypt is almost synonymous with the Pyramids of Gizeh, the Sphinx and the Valley of the Tombs of the Kings. Photographs illustrating the glamour of that old civilization along the Nile may fill the void left by the silence of the records concerning the Hebrews from Joseph to Moses. These four hundred years are covered by only three Bible verses.[4] Had the Hebrews, even in the time of Joseph, traveled a little farther south, they would have viewed with much the same interest as modern tourists the Pyramids and the huge Sphinx, representing an age even then almost a thousand years old.

The upper picture shows the familiar Sphinx bathed in the slanting mellow rays of the setting sun. Combining the body of a lion with a head representing the ancient Pharaoh Khafre, the Sphinx towers almost seventy feet above the relentless sand of the desert and extends 190 feet at the base. Visible beyond is the great Pyramid of Khufu,[5] the largest of the Pyramids, constructed approximately 2500 B.C. as a tomb for the Pharaoh.

The lower photograph takes us four hundred miles south to Thebes,[6] the capital of Egypt before and after the rule of the Hyksos. There, from above the entrance to the great Temple of Karnak, guarded by rows of ram-headed sphinxes, we look west across the Nile to the cliffs overlooking the Valley of the Tombs of the Kings. From that valley have come some of the most fabulous objects of the ancient world.

Many monuments still standing in Egypt today are mute evidence of the slavery the Hebrews and other peoples endured throughout the Empire period,[7] which followed the expulsion of the Hyksos. It was into this period of fabulous construction by extravagant kings at the expense of countless human lives that Moses came to present to the world a new vision rooted in faith.

---

[1] Genesis 47: 11.
[2] Genesis 42-46.
[3] Genesis 47: 1-12.

[4] Exodus 1: 6-8.
[5] Also called by the Greek name *Cheops*.

[6] No or No-Amon in some Bibles; near modern Luxor.
[7] About 1550-1250 B.C.

a. The desert of Sinai east of Suez, probably the southern edge of the Wilderness of Shur.

b. The Oasis of 'Ayun Musa 12 miles south of Suez along the probable route of the Exodus.

c. The interior of Sinai at Serabit el-Khadim (biblical Dophkah?).

[Plate 6]

Flight from Egypt

(Sinai Peninsula)

¶ *But God led the people round by the way of the wilderness toward the Red Sea [literally, Sea of Reeds]. And the people of Israel went up out of the land of Egypt...*[1]
¶ *When Israel was a child, I loved him, and out of Egypt I called my son.*[2]
¶ *By faith the people crossed the Red Sea as if on dry land...*[3]

THE escape from oppression and bondage in Egypt, the victory at the Red Sea (or, Sea of Reeds), and the experience at Mount Sinai crystallized the early foundation of biblical faith. It was in this momentous Exodus under the leadership of Moses that subsequent writers — storytellers, prophets, psalmists, and early Christians — saw the hand of God at work in history. Their faith was kindled.

The annual Passover festival has kept the Exodus vivid in Jewish memory.

Moses, skilled and hardened by many years of desert life, led his people with patience down through the Wilderness of Shur,[4] along the coast of Sinai and into the rugged mountains near the southern tip. The pictures of that route shown here illustrate the main features of the Sinai Peninsula in which the Hebrews spent more than a generation.

The upper photograph looks west from the rolling sand dunes of the desert east of modern Suez, at the head of the Gulf of Suez shimmering in the distance at the left. Here was the southern portion of the Wilderness of Shur. Vast stretches of similar wilderness lay ahead of the fleeing Hebrews.

The ceaseless search for fresh water in such country, the burning heat of the sun with no shade for relief, the shifting, penetrating sands, leave small wonder that the Hebrew slaves from the rich Valley of the Nile were restless and fearful under Moses' guidance.[5]

The middle picture illustrates the welcome contrast that must have greeted the weary Hebrews when a desert oasis appeared before them. Though not identified with any place mentioned in the Bible, this oasis, called 'Ayun Musa,[6] lay along the probable route followed by the Hebrews. The deep blue Gulf of Suez can be seen through the trees in the background.

Below is a view of the interior of Sinai, looking east from Serabit el-Khadim, the center of the ancient Egyptian turquoise mines. For over a thousand years these mines had supplied precious stones for royal jewelry. Here, perhaps, was located biblical Dophkah.[7] The wide valley in the distance is the Wadi Serabit, which may have been the Wilderness of Sin.[8] Some forty-five miles southeast rise the high peaks among which is famed Mount Sinai.

---

[1] Exodus 13: 18.
[2] Hosea 11: 1.
[3] Hebrews 11: 29.

[4] Exodus 15: 22 ff.
[5] Exodus 32; Numbers 11.
[6] "Springs of Moses."

[7] Numbers 33: 12.
[8] Exodus 16; Numbers 33: 11.

St. Catherine's Monastery near Mount Sinai, today called Jebel Musa, "Mountain of Moses."
[Plate 7]

Covenant at Mount Sinai

(Mount Sinai)

¶ *When they . . . came into the wilderness
of Sinai, they encamped in the wilderness; and
there Israel encamped before the mountain.
And Moses went up to God, and the LORD
called him out of the mountain, saying, "Thus
shall you say to the house of Jacob, ..."*[1]

DEEPLY embedded in the story of hardships suffered by the
Hebrews during their wanderings in Sinai was the establish-
ment of the Covenant at Mount Sinai.[2] There the giving of
the Law fused into the hearts of the people an objective that was for
all of life and for every age.

Faith in God molds the character of
man's relations to his fellow men. Thus
the giving of the Ten Commandments
at Mount Sinai established a foundation for faith and its expression in right
relations among all men.

Though seldom has man perfectly
measured up to the standards God has
set for him, the story of the Law at
Sinai remains an unforgettable reminder of that which God intends. In the
Ten Commandments one finds the simple, irreducible minimum of the expression of faith. Without basic moral
laws there can be no hope for peace
within any group or between nations.

Since the 4th century A.D. a small
group of Greek Orthodox monks have
lived near the foot of Mount Sinai
in Saint Catherine's Monastery. They
symbolize the faith which brought the
Hebrews there and the Law which they
took away with them to the Holy Land.
In this monastery far removed from
civilization, in the rigorous climate of
the high altitudes of the barren mountains surrounding them, the monks have
gathered a vast library of ancient

manuscripts. Among these Tischendorf
found in 1843 the famed *Codex Sinaiti-
cus*, a 4th century Greek Bible, now
the proud possession of the British Museum. Expeditions have periodically
visited the monastery to explore its treas-
ures. In 1949 all important manuscripts
in this library were carefully micro-
filmed to make them available to the
world of biblical scholarship.

The lofty, rugged, barren cliffs of the
mountain masses, towering sharply
above the little monastery, give silent
testimony to the spiritual experience
more than three thousand years ago.
It provided a bond of unity for a restless group of Hebrews who had been
slaves amid the extravagant splendor of
one of the most powerful nations of
the ancient world. Already declining
when Moses appeared, the splendor of
that Egyptian civilization remains today only in gradually crumbling monuments to vain and despotic kings. But
the faith that was sparked at Sinai with
simple laws of living continues to stir
the hearts of men and mold their character toward a better civilization.

---

[1] Exodus 19: 2-3.   [2] Exodus 19-20, 24.

a. The Jordan River at the traditional site where the Hebrews crossed under Joshua.

b. The Plain of the Jordan, looking south from the mound of ancient Jericho.

c. The northwest edge of the Dead Sea with the plateau of Transjordan in the distance.

[Plate 8]

C. 1250 B.C.

Crossing the Jordan
(River Jordan — Jericho)

⁋ *So, when the people set out from their tents, to pass over the Jordan. . . the waters coming down from above stood and rose up in a heap far off, at Adam. . . and those flowing down toward the sea of the Arabah, the Salt Sea, were wholly cut off; and the people passed over opposite Jericho.*[1]

A GENERATION passed before the Hebrews emerged from their desert wanderings to view the Land of Canaan from the banks of the muddy River Jordan. Commemorated in song and poetry, the River Jordan and the city of Jericho are probably as well known as any other places in the Holy Land.

Some twenty-five miles north of the Dead Sea, near the point where the Jabbok River from Gilead joins the Jordan at Adam,[2] the waters were dammed up for a while, allowing the river to drain below. Thus the Hebrews crossed easily into the plain east of Jericho.

Already God had saved them once when water blocked their way, as the Egyptians pressed down upon them.[3] In this incident once again the Hebrews saw evidence of His work in history, and their faith increased.

The upper picture shows the muddy, swiftly flowing Jordan at a point about four miles north of its entrance into the Dead Sea and not unlikely the site of the ancient crossing. Several Christian monasteries stand close by this spot, which tradition also designates as the place where Jesus was baptized by John many centuries later.[4]

The fortified Canaanite city of Jericho then faced the Hebrews. The mound of earth and rubble in the foreground of the middle picture remains as mute evidence that they surmounted that obstacle. Excavations of Tell es-Sultan, which lies on the northwest edge of modern Jericho, have revealed exciting remains of ancient pre-Hebrew culture. It is now apparent that the debris of the Canaanite city destroyed by Joshua was washed and blown away in ancient times. As the digging continues there, however, new evidence may yet be uncovered.

In the picture we are looking south across a banana orchard and the Plain of the Jordan to the point where the eastern plateau of the Wilderness of Judah drops off sharply to the Dead Sea, almost 1300 feet below sea level. The mound of earth at the extreme right was recently found to be the Jericho of New Testament times.

In the lower picture the northern end of the Dead Sea (or Salt Sea) is seen against the hills of Ammon and Moab. Rising steeply to form the eastern edge of the Great Rift through which the Jordan flows, they provide a natural barrier between Palestine and Transjordan. The name *Dead Sea* aptly describes the highly saline water in which no living creatures can exist.

[1] Joshua 3: 14, 16.
[2] Modern Tell Damiya.
[3] Exodus 14.
[4] Mark 1; see page 49.

a. The modern village of Jib, the site of ancient Gibeon at the head of the Valley of Aijalon.

b. The upper end of the Valley of Aijalon where Joshua's army defeated the Amorites.

[Plate 9]

Conquest of the Highlands

(GIBEON — VALLEY OF AIJALON)

¶ *Then Joshua gathered all the tribes of Israel to Shechem, . . . and they presented themselves before God. And Joshua said to all the people, ". . . fear the LORD, and serve him in sincerity and in faithfulness; . . . choose this day whom you will serve, . . . as for me and my house, we will serve the LORD."*[1]

ONCE Jericho was captured, the formidable barrier of the highland country to the west, with its fortified Amorite (or Canaanite) cities, faced the Hebrews. Ascending through the deep, treacherous ravines of the rugged wilderness region[2] from Jericho, the Hebrews pressed upon Ai[3] and Bethel.[4]

At Mount Ebal[5] Joshua gathered the people together to renew their covenant with the LORD. There they promised to obey the Law.[6] Then gradually they worked their way south along the central highlands.

The Gibeonites made peace without a battle,[7] but Joshua faced a coalition of Amorite kings near Gibeon. It was during the rout of those kings in the Valley of Aijalon that Joshua prayed for the sun to stay in the heavens to lengthen the day.[8]

In the upper photograph the little village of Jib (ancient Gibeon) commands a view of the plain in which the battle began. The road which passes to the right, in the foreground of the picture, leads west to the Valley of Aijalon. The lower scene shows the rugged, rocky ravine that forms the upper end of the valley at the edge of the plain. Down this ravine the fleeing Amorites scrambled, with the army of Joshua in hot pursuit.

The conquest of the country proceeded slowly, as the Book of Judges implies. Each Hebrew tribe had to gain its own foothold. The process apparently continued for about two centuries (c. 1250 — c. 1050 B.C.).

At Shechem, however, Joshua had impressed upon the tribes the necessity for unity in faith and loyalty to God[9] with the words, "choose this day whom you will serve." The sacred Ark, containing the tablets of the Law as a symbol of God's presence, was housed at Shiloh, the center of worship,[10] about eleven miles south of Shechem in the central highlands.

The pictures of Gibeon and the Valley of Aijalon illustrate also the contest between the followers of David and those of Saul two centuries later.[11] To Gibeon Solomon came to offer sacrifice and prayer prior to building the Temple in Jerusalem.[12] Through this same valley many centuries later (168 B.C.) Judas Maccabeus chased the army of Antiochus Epiphanes,[13] ushering in a brief period of Jewish independence.[14]

---

[1] Joshua 24: 1a, c; 2a; 14a; 15b, d.
[2] See plate 12c.
[3] Modern et-Tell.
[4] Modern Beitin; Joshua 7-8.
[5] See plate 2b.
[6] Joshua 8: 30-35.
[7] Joshua 9.
[8] Joshua 10: 12.
[9] Joshua 24.
[10] Modern Seilun; Joshua 18: 1; 1 Samuel 1-3.
[11] 2 Samuel 2.
[12] 1 Kings 3.
[13] 1 Maccabees 3: 13-24.
[14] See page 47.

a. Looking west from Tell es-Safi (biblical Libnah?) across the Philistine Plain.

b. Sowing and plowing wheat on Tell er-Rumeileh (biblical Beth Shemesh).

c. Qaryat el-'Inab (Kiriath-jearim?) in the Judean highlands west of Jerusalem.

[Plate 10]

Facing a New Foe

(Beth Shemesh — Kiriath-jearim)

¶ *Then Samuel said to all the house of Israel, "If you are returning to the* Lord *with all your heart, then put away the foreign gods and the Ashtaroth from among you, and direct your heart to the* Lord, *and serve him only, and he will deliver you out of the hand of the Philistines."*[1]

HAVING gained control of the highlands, the Hebrews faced a new foe to the west — the Philistines.[2] They had come across the sea from the island of Crete to settle along the Mediterranean coast. The struggle for domination of the Holy Land between these new invaders and the Hebrews continued for over a century.

The upper picture is a view of the Philistine Plain, looking west toward the Mediterranean from Tell es-Safi, which may have been the ancient biblical city of Libnah.[3] The fall plowing of the fertile plain had just been completed when the picture was taken.

The center and lower photographs illustrate the story of the first clash between the Hebrews and the Philistines, when the sacred Ark of the Covenant was captured.[4] It had been taken into battle with the hope that its presence would assure the Hebrews victory. The Philistines later returned the Ark to Beth Shemesh,[5] the remains of which lie beneath the ground being sown and plowed in the center photograph.

The broad Valley of Sorek, famed for the exploits of Samson and Delilah,[6] forms the background of the mound and opens out into the Philistine Plain at left. The oxen are reminiscent of the cows chosen by the Philistines to haul the Ark, with a box full of golden mice and tumors, to Beth Shemesh. From there it was taken into the highland country to Kiriath-jearim, where it remained in the house of Abinadab until taken to Jerusalem by David twenty or more years later.[7]

The lower photograph shows the modern village of Qaryat el-'Inab (Abu Ghosh) from the hill to its west. Nearby is a Christian church with a statue of the Virgin mounted above an ark on the rooftop and believed to be the site of the home of Abinadab.

The prominent building in the foreground is a beautifully preserved Crusader church, now part of a Dominican monastery. Beside it was recently discovered an ancient Roman caravansary, the ancient counterpart of a modern motel. At the extreme left in the photograph the modern highway winds its way eastward to Jerusalem some eight miles away among the hills on the horizon. The round hill at right, with its cluster of houses on top, is modern Suba, which suggests that "a city set on a hill cannot be hid."[8]

---

[1] 1 Samuel 7: 3.
[2] The name "Palestine" originated from the Greek form of "Philistine."
[3] Joshua 10: 29.
[4] 1 Samuel 4: 1-7: 4.
[5] Modern Tell er-Rumeileh.
[6] Judges 16: 4.
[7] 2 Samuel 6.
[8] Matthew 5: 14.

a. Tell en-Nasbeh, six miles north of Jerusalem, probably the Mizpah of Samuel.

b. The mosque of the modern village of Nabi Samwil, believed to surmount the tomb of Samuel.

c. The modern village of Bira (biblical Beeroth?), southwest of ancient Bethel.

[Plate 11]

The Need for Unity

(Mizpah — Beeroth)

¶ Samuel judged Israel all the days of his life. And he went on a circuit year by year to Bethel, Gilgal, and Mizpah; . . . Then he would come back to Ramah, for his home was there, and there also he administered justice to Israel.[1]

IN SAMUEL, the last of the Judges, the Hebrews found a man who, without making claims to rule as a king, came nearest to achieving their ideal of a state ruled by God through a religious leader. The scattered tribes of the highlands accomplished through him a certain degree of unity in faith. The Philistines were pressing hard from the west. A unifying spirit was essential if what the Hebrews had gained for their faith was to be preserved.

Samuel lived and worked in the territory of Benjamin, just north of Jerusalem and illustrated in the photographs. The identity of some of the places is quite uncertain. Considerable debate has raged over the location of Mizpah (where the activities of Samuel centered at first)[2] since the excavation of Tell en-Nasbeh, the mound in the upper picture. This site is about six miles north of Jerusalem. Here was found a strongly fortified city with tremendous walls and a complex gate. The discovery of a clay seal impression of Gedaliah (whose brief rule at Mizpah, many years after Samuel, ended in tragedy)[3] added to the conviction that here was ancient Mizpah.

The rival site for Mizpah, Nabi Samwil, is a small village atop a high hill four miles northwest of Jerusalem and is visible for miles around. Its most prominent building is the mosque with a tall minaret (center photograph), be-lieved to be built over the tomb of Samuel. The name *Nabi Samwil* means "the Prophet Samuel." Thus tradition associates this place with one of the cities frequented by the prophet-judge.

The lower picture shows the modern village of Bira (perhaps biblical Beeroth),[4] just north of Tell en-Nasbeh. Samuel must have passed this way many times as he went from Mizpah to Bethel, which lies a short distance northeast over the hill and beyond the horizon. Ancient Ramah, the home of Samuel, lay at Er-Ram about four miles to the south of Bira.

The location of Gilgal is very uncertain. Was it the site near the Jordan where the Hebrews had first camped on entering the country?[5] Or was it in the highland country of Ephraim? There is a Jiljiliya today, about nine miles north of Bira and five miles north of Jifna,[6] which some scholars identify with ancient Gilgal.

---

[1] 1 Samuel 7: 15-17.
[2] 1 Samuel 7: 5ff.
[3] 2 Kings 25: 22ff; Jeremiah 40-41.
[4] 2 Samuel 4: 2.
[5] Joshua 4: 19.
[6] See plate 2a.

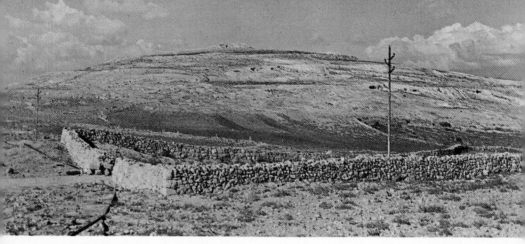

a. Tell el-Ful, site of ancient Gibeah, capital of the United Kingdom under Saul.

b. Excavated remains of some of the masonry that formed the fortress atop Gibeah.

c. Looking east from Gibeah across the wilderness to the Jordan Valley.

[Plate 12]

Unity Achieved Under Saul

(GIBEAH — ANATHOTH)

¶ Then Samuel told the people the rights and duties of the kingship; and he wrote them in a book and laid it up before the LORD. *Then Samuel sent all the people away, ... Saul also went to his home at Gibeah, and with him went men of valor whose hearts God had touched.*[1]

SAMUEL feared that to establish a throne over his people might destroy the foundation of their unity in religious faith. The people, however, wanted strength to meet their common foe, the Philistines; and they sought a king who could command their allegiance and unite their physical strength.[2] Thus Saul was chosen and anointed king by Samuel at Mizpah.[3]

The act of anointing indicated only that he was serving in behalf of God. (The Hebrew word meaning "to anoint" is the root from which comes the word *Messiah,* literally "Anointed One." In Greek it is *Christos.*)[4]

For a while, at least, Saul did succeed in mustering the tribes together against the Philistines; but many years passed before they were subdued.

The photographs reveal Saul's wisdom in his choice of Gibeah for a capital. It was the highest point in the area, about three miles north of Jerusalem (then a city of the Jebusites), giving the inhabitants the best possible protection against their enemies. Gibeah means "height" in Hebrew. The upper picture, looking northeast, gives a view of the conical hill, today called Tell el-Ful,[5] with some remains of ancient Gibeah still visible.

The center photograph shows a section of the pile of debris at the summit of the hill after it was excavated by Dr. W. F. Albright during three campaigns. The particular wall shown was probably part of a later reconstruction of Saul's citadel, for Gibeah remained an important outpost even after Jerusalem became the capital,[6] about thirty years later. In Maccabean times a prosperous city occupied this hill.

The lower scene reveals the excellent view commanded by Saul's fortress at Gibeah. Looking toward the east one can see the barren, rocky wilderness sloping off to the deep Valley of the Jordan. The thin ribbon of the river valley appears faintly about eighteen miles away. A portion of the Dead Sea can be seen beyond the last ridge. The small village of 'Anata lies at the right in the photograph near the ancient site of Anathoth, Jeremiah's home town.[7]

Gibeah and Anathoth lay astride the route of the Assyrian army which approached Jerusalem in 701 B.C.[8]

---

[1] 1 Samuel 10: 25-26.
[2] 1 Samuel 8.
[3] 1 Samuel 10.
[4] See pages 47 and 51.
[5] Literally "hill of horse beans."
[6] See page 29.
[7] Jeremiah 1: 1; 32: 6-15.
[8] Isaiah 10: 27-34; see page 37.

a. Tell Zakariya (biblical Azekah) which guards the entrance to the Vale of Elah

b. The Vale of Elah, scene of David's encounter with Goliath, viewed from the Tell.

c. Mount Gilboa, the northern end of the central highlands, from across the Plain of Esdraelon.

[Plate 13]

Disunity and Strife

(VALE OF ELAH — MOUNT GILBOA)

¶ . . . *Samuel grieved over Saul. And the*
LORD *repented that he had made Saul king
over Israel.*[1]
¶ *"Saul has slain his thousands,
And David his ten thousands."*[2]
¶ *"Thy glory, O Israel, is slain upon thy
high places!
How are the mighty fallen!"*[3]

SAUL had not been king long when the fears of Samuel concerning the anointing of a king began to be realized. The "divine right of kings" began to overshadow the divine responsibility of God's anointed. Samuel became discouraged. Saul grew mentally ill. David was brought to soothe the king with music.

When, however, the women of Gibeah sang of the great prowess of David in battle and belittled Saul, jealousy flared. David fled, but not until he had cemented a deep friendship with Saul's son Jonathan.[4] Amid the disunity, David gathered together a group of followers who became the nucleus for a kingdom later to be reunited.

The Philistine menace continued with a decisive battle on Mount Gilboa in which Saul and Jonathan were slain.[5] David's lament over these two determined warriors is one of the classics of early Hebrew poetry.[6]

Illustrating this graphic period of Hebrew history, the pictures show, first, the entrance to the Vale of Elah in the foothills (called the Shephelah) of the Judean highlands. At the left towers the hill on which a fortress (ancient Azekah), stood to guard the valley in which the Philistines encamped.[7] In the distance at the right Tell es-Safi[8] is visible on the edge of the Philistine Plain.

The top of Azekah (today called Tell Zakariya) in the center picture commands an excellent view of the hills to the south. Among them were many biblical cities which Micah graphically portrayed years later in his dynamic sermon.[9] Spreading out below is the Vale of Elah (valley of the terebinth), scene of David's encounter with the Philistine giant Goliath.

The lower photograph takes us far north to the Plain of Esdraelon,[10] at the southeastern edge of which rises Mount Gilboa, the northern end of the mountains of Samaria in the central highlands. Appearing blue in the distant haze, Mount Gilboa contrasts sharply with the rich green of the fertile plain which has witnessed many a contest for control of its productive soil.[11]

At the extreme left in this picture is Sulam (Shunem of 1 Samuel 28: 4 and 2 Kings 4: 8), located on the lower edge of the hill of Moreh.[12] At the foot of Mount Gilboa is modern Zir'in, ancient Jezreel of the story of Ahab and Naboth's vineyard.[13]

---

[1] 1 Samuel 15: 35.
[2] 1 Samuel 18: 7b.
[3] 2 Samuel 1: 19.
[4] 1 Samuel 19-20.
[5] 1 Samuel 31.
[6] 2 Samuel 1: 19-27.
[7] 1 Samuel 17: 1.
[8] See plate 10a.
[9] Micah 1: 10-16.
[10] The 'Emeq.
[11] See plates 18b and 23b.
[12] See plate 23b.
[13] 1 Kings 21.

a. Looking north across the Valley of Hinnom to the site of ancient Jerusalem.

b. The City of David (center) from the east side of the Valley of the Kidron.

[Plate 14]

A New Center for Rule and Worship

(JERUSALEM — CITY OF DAVID)

¶ And David and all Israel went to Jerusalem, that is Jebus, where the Jebusites were, ... And David dwelt in the stronghold; therefore it was called the city of David.[1]

FOR a brief time after the death of Saul, his son Ishbosheth ruled in the north, while David was anointed king over Judah at Hebron.[2] Soon David gained the upper hand. To fuse the people more firmly together, he captured Jerusalem, a stronghold of the Jebusites and therefore neutral territory, and made it his capital.[3]

He united the people also in worship by removing the sacred Ark of the Covenant from the house of Abinadab at Kiriath-jearim[4] and placing it in a tent sanctuary in the center of the new capital.[5] A period of expansion followed as David succeeded in pushing the Philistines back to a narrow strip along the southern sea coast.

Although the western hill of Jerusalem is today referred to as Zion's Hill, it is now known that the City of David[6] was on the eastern slope adjacent to the Valley of the Kidron.[7] The upper picture, looking north from across the Valley of Hinnom (often called Gehinnom), shows the Temple site dominating the horizon, with a hill sloping off sharply to the right into the Valley of the Kidron. It was on this slope, which with a few scattered houses today lies outside the city wall, that the original City of David was built.

In the foreground the luxuriant fig orchard is probably the location of the ancient "King's Garden," through which many years later King Zedekiah and his men fled as the Babylonians seized Jerusalem in 587 B.C.[8] The village of Silwan (biblical Siloam) clings to the hill on the right, behind which is the Mount of Olives.

The lower photograph looks northwest from the village of Silwan toward the ancient City of David directly in the center. Just beneath the dome of the Mosque el Aksa, which dominates the horizon, a portion of the ancient Jebusite wall of Jerusalem is still exposed. Lower down, beside the Kidron Valley to the right, is the spring Gihon.[9] This spring was the main water supply of ancient Jerusalem. The original conduits still run from it to the Siloam pool (left center, by the minaret[10]) and to the Upper Pool,[11] which is thought to be the Birket el Hamra (obscured by the trees) farther left.

The Valley of the Tyropoeon (Cheese makers' Valley), upper left in the picture, separates the City of David from the western hill. At one time this debris-filled valley was fifty or more feet deeper than it is now.

---

[1] 1 Chronicles 11: 4, 7.
[2] See plate 3b.
[3] 2 Samuel 5: 6-10.
[4] See plate 10c and page 21.
[5] 2 Samuel 6.
[6] Also called Ophel, 2 Chronicles 27: 3; 33: 14.
[7] See plates 1 and 26a.
[8] 2 Kings 25: 4.
[9] Also called the Virgin's Fountain.
[10] 2 Kings 20: 20; Nehemiah 3: 15.
[11] Isaiah 7: 3.

a. Some of the lofty cedars of Lebanon in the small grove east of Tripoli.
b. Air view of Sidon pressed against the rugged range of the Lebanon Mountains.

c. The Dome of the Rock which rises over the huge rock where Solomon's Temple once stood.

[Plate 15]

The Golden Age

(JERUSALEM — HOLY CITY)

¶ *Then Solomon said,*
"The LORD has set the sun in the heavens,
  but has said that he would dwell in
    thick darkness.
I have built thee an exalted house,
  a place for thee to dwell in for ever."[1]

DAVID'S brilliant and skilled leadership produced a period of peace and prosperity in the Holy Land, a period rightly described as the Golden Age of Hebrew history. The crowning achievement of that age was the construction of the Temple, which quickly became the focal point of the growing faith.

David had hoped to build the Temple, but he succeeded only in choosing its site, the threshing floor of Araunah, which lay above the city to the north.[2] Later tradition claims it also as Mount Moriah, where Abraham had offered to sacrifice his son Isaac.[3]

It remained for Solomon to build the Temple, which he proceeded to do with great elaboration.[4] He hired the best workmen, skilled artisans from Syria to the north. Great quantities of cedar and cypress timbers from the mountains of Lebanon were brought down to the coast, made into rafts and floated to a convenient point opposite Jerusalem. Huge blocks of stone were cut to provide the foundation, and thousands of details were worked out with meticulous care. At the dedication of the Temple Solomon prayed that it might be a symbol of God's concern for all peoples.[5]

Today the only living link with that ancient Temple is an occasional small grove of rugged cedars in the mountains of Lebanon. One of these majestic trees is shown here from the famous grove of about four hundred trees located east of Tripoli. Plate 15b gives an air view farther south, showing the rugged peaks of the Lebanons which form a backdrop for the city of Sidon. From there, perhaps, the great log rafts were launched.

Not a stone or fragment from Solomon's Temple remains at its site in Jerusalem today to tell the story of its grandeur. Perhaps a few original stones lie beneath the Wailing Wall on the west side of the Temple enclosure. The vicissitudes of the centuries that followed the Golden Age erased the last vestige of the Temple's glory. All that remains is the native rock of Araunah's threshing floor, enshrined beneath the beautiful Dome of the Rock.[6]

In the lower picture we see the Dome framed in the olive trees gracing the eastern area of what is today called the Haram esh-Sharif ("The Noble Sanctuary"). The huge rock beneath the Dome remains the symbol of the faith which first prompted its choice for a temple to God.

---

[1] 1 Kings 8: 12-13.
[2] 2 Samuel 24: 18-25.
[3] Genesis 22.
[4] 1 Kings 5-7.
[5] 1 Kings 8: 41-43.
[6] See *Frontispiece* and plate 30.

a. The spring at ʿEin Fariʿa north of Nablus, looking east toward the Jordan Valley.

b. Tell Fariʿa, perhaps ancient Tirzah, being excavated by the French Dominican school of archeology.

[Plate 16]

Disunity Again and Finally

(Tirzah)

¶ *And when all Israel saw that the king did not hearken to them, the people answered the king,*
"What portion have we in David?
We have no inheritance in the son of Jesse.
To your tents, O Israel!
Look now to your own house, David."

THE evidences of Solomon's great building program are gradually coming to light as excavators uncover the remains of ancient cities in the Holy Land. In all his building Solomon failed to consider that it was human lives that made up his kingdom — not just timber, stones and mortar.[2] Oriental despotism had crept in as his wealth, power and influence increased.

After his death the people demanded of Rehoboam, his son, release from their burdens. The young king shunned the wise counsel of the elders: "If you will be a servant to this people today . . . they will be your servants for ever."[3] Under Jeroboam the northern tribes revolted with the cry, "To your tents, O Israel!" The kingdom was split, never to be healed again.

The struggle between the North and South continued for over a hundred years thereafter. Jeroboam began to fortify cities in the north — Shechem, Penuel, Tirzah — and established centers of worship at Dan and Bethel.[4]

In the upper photograph the goats, sheep, oxen, and men peacefully gather to drink of the copious water from the spring at 'Ein-Fari'a a few miles northeast of Shechem,[5] in the heart of Jeroboam's kingdom. Meanwhile, nearby, excavators dig into a large hill shown in the lower view. Here Dominican Fathers, skilled archeologists from Jerusalem, direct the excavation of Tell Fari'a, thought to be the site of ancient Tirzah, Jeroboam's capital.

The process of excavation is slow and tedious, often going on for many weeks with little to show for the effort. Layer by layer is gradually removed, everything being carefully photographed and recorded before anything is destroyed to dig deeper. Each level below the one above reveals an older period of the city's history. The level exposed in the foreground of this picture is called the Middle Bronze Age, an important period of this Canaanite city which flourished in the time of Abraham.

The workmen were just beginning to dig into the higher levels on the left as this picture was taken in 1947. There they found remains from the time of Jeroboam (Iron Age I). Was this Jeroboam's capital at Tirzah? After many seasons of work that question is still unanswered, but the evidence tends toward the affirmative.

---

[1] 1 Kings 12: 16.
[2] 1 Kings 5: 13-18.
[3] 1 Kings 12: 7.
[4] 1 Kings 12: 25-33; 14: 17.
[5] See plates 2b, 4bc and 25b.

a. Site of Omri's capital of Samaria as it appears from the south.

b. Remains of a section of Omri's wall around Samaria (c. 850 B.C.).

c. Fragments of carved ivory from the palace of Jeroboam II at Samaria.

[Plate 17]

Voices of Warning

(SAMARIA)

¶ *"Woe to those who are at ease in Zion,
and to those who feel secure on
the mountain of Samaria, . . ."*
¶ *"Woe to those who lie upon beds of ivory,
and stretch themselves upon their
couches, . . ."*[1]

TWO turbulent centuries followed the division of the Kingdom.[2] Shishak of Egypt invaded Palestine[3] as war broke out between Israel and Judah. Samaria was built by Omri for his capital.[4] Religious conflict with idolatrous Canaanite Baalism reached a climax during the reign of Omri's son, Ahab, as a result of the dynamic influence of the Hebrew prophets Elijah and Elisha.[5]

Brief periods of peace and prosperity had been enjoyed, but a longer period came under Jeroboam II in Israel and Uzziah in Judah about 800 to 750 B.C. With peace, wealth accumulated and social upheaval followed. Faith became weakened by religious pomp, indifference and apostasy.

The heritage of the old Covenant faith, not easily forgotten, called forth new voices of warning. These were the writing prophets of Israel and Judah: Amos, Hosea, Isaiah and Micah. The people were reminded that peace and prosperity are the gifts of God and carry with them the obligation of sincere faith expressed in moral living. Faith requires more than outward observance. God looks to the heart of man:

*"He has showed you, O man, what is good;
and what does the LORD require of you
but to do justice, and to love kindness,
and to walk humbly with your God?"*[6]

The cultural developments of these two centuries are gradually being pieced together as the sites of ancient cities are explored. A few miles north of Nablus one is impressed with the stratagem of Omri in his choice of Samaria[7] for a capital, as the great mound suddenly springs into view. From the south one sees (upper picture) at the highest point some of the remains of the ancient acropolis, first built by Omri but later rebuilt and enlarged.

In the center picture a small section of the foundation of Omri's southeastern wall is seen exposed. Most of the remains visible to the modern visitor are from the Greek, Roman, and early Christian times.

The lower picture vividly illustrates the famed Ivory Palace[8] mentioned as one of the achievements of Ahab. These elaborate ivory carvings, however, were from the period of Jeroboam II, during whose reign Amos preached against "those who lie upon beds of ivory." Combining the art of Phoenicia and Egypt, the carvings were imported by the rulers and the wealthy for inlays in furniture and wall panels.

---

[1] Amos 6: 1a, 4a.
[2] 1 Kings 14: 21 —
2 Kings 14: 22.
[3] c. 920 B.C.
[4] c. 875 B.C.
[5] c. 860 B.C.
[6] Micah 6: 8.
[7] Modern Sebastiya.
[8] 1 Kings 22: 39.

a. A vineyard with a watchtower in the hill country of Ephraim south of modern Nablus.

b. The Plain of Esdraelon (Armageddon) from atop Tell el-Mutesellim (ancient Megiddo).

[Plate 18]

Living by Faith

(Vineyard — Megiddo)

¶ *I will take my stand to watch,
    and station myself on the tower,
    and look forth to see what he
        will say to me, . . .*[1]
¶ *Yet I planted you a choice vine,
    wholly of pure seed.
    How then have you turned degenerate
    and become a wild vine?*[2]

THE 8th-century prophets left their indelible stamp of faith on all subsequent generations. Time and again they were proved right. Assyria swallowed up Israel as Samaria fell to Sargon.[3] Judah, consisting of only a small portion of the Holy Land, was attacked and devastated by Sennacherib.[4] Surrounded by hostile powers, Judah paid heavy tribute for the little freedom she could enjoy.

In fear King Manasseh succumbed to a period of placating foreign rulers and worshiping foreign gods. Thus the first half of the 7th century became the Dark Ages of Judah's history.[5]

Those loyal to the faith secretly turned to writing. Then the great reform of Josiah in 621 brought forth new hope, only to be dashed when Josiah was slain at Megiddo as Egypt sallied forth to help the defeated Assyrian army.[6] Prophetic voices — Jeremiah (ch. 12), Habakkuk (1, 2), and Ezekiel (18) — queried, "Why do the righteous suffer?" Had not Josiah been the most righteous king in centuries?" "The righteous shall live by his faith,"[7] was the only answer. Nothing else mattered.

A frequent reference, both in symbol and in fact, is made in Scripture to the vineyard, one of the main resources of the Holy Land both then and now. The tragedy over Naboth's Vineyard, seized by Ahab, provoked the invective of Elijah.[8] Isaiah's Song of the Vineyard is one of the classics of Hebrew poetry.[9] Habakkuk mounted the tower, characteristic of every vineyard (upper picture), as he sought an answer to his theological dilemma. A vineyard was the setting for a parable of Jesus.[10]

From the mound of Megiddo (lower picture), on which a few of the remains of the ancient fortified city can be seen, we look northeast across the plain of Esdraelon to Mount Tabor, where Deborah and Barak had gathered the Hebrews together[11] and where one tradition says the Transfiguration of Jesus occurred.[12] The River Kishon[13] winds across the plain, where Jehu raced his chariot during his campaign to rid the country of Baalism.[14] Here Josiah was slain. Here, too, many believe the last great battle of the world will be fought — at "Armageddon."[15]

---

[1] Habakkuk 2: 1.
[2] Jeremiah 2: 21.
[3] 721 B.C.; 2 Kings 17: 1-6.
[4] 701 B.C.; 2 Kings 18-19.
[5] 2 Kings 21.
[6] 609 B.C.; 2 Kings 22-23.
[7] Habakkuk 2: 4.
[8] 1 Kings 21; see page 27.
[9] Isaiah 5: 1-7.
[10] Mark 12: 1-12.
[11] Judges 4: 6, 14.
[12] Mark 9: 2-13.
[13] Judges 4-5.
[14] 2 Kings 9.
[15] Revelation 16: 16; see plates 13c and 23b.

a. Remains of the fortifications of the ancient city of Lachish (Tell ed-Duweir).

b. Remains of the outer gate reveal signs of devastation by the Babylonian army.

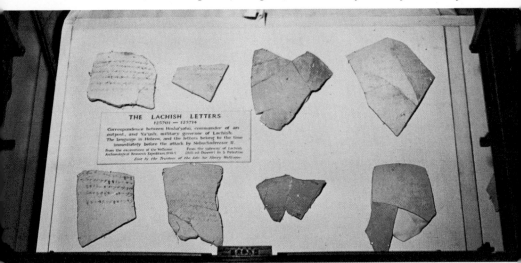

c. Some of the "Lachish Letters" found in a guard room just inside the gate.

[Plate 19]

"By the Waters of Babylon"

(LACHISH)

¶ How lonely sits the city
that was full of people!
How like a widow has she become,
she that was great among the nations![1]

IF the death of Josiah was difficult for the Hebrew people to equate with their faith, the fall of Jerusalem in 587 was a complete dilemma. The prophets had been right, painfully right! The Babylonians under Nebuchadnezzar moved westward about 600.

Jehoiachin, King of Judah, having succeeded his father, Jehoiakim, a mere three months, capitulated in 598 and was taken off to Babylon. The Holy City was spared, and Zedekiah placed on the throne. At first loyal to Babylon, he soon began to play politics with Egypt.

Again Nebuchadnezzar moved west, this time with destructive intent. His ruthless armies leveled city after city in Judah. The final stroke saw Jerusalem reduced to rubble.[2] With the Holy City destroyed by pagans and its leaders taken into exile, all hope was gone. Faith succumbed to a mood of despair "by the waters of Babylon."[3]

The grim evidence of those painful years is clearly written beneath the soil of many a mound in the Holy Land. Such evidences in Jerusalem have long since been erased, but the graphic witness to those days has been uncovered at Tell ed-Duweir. A huge mound in the southern Shephelah, it was the site of ancient Lachish.

Already this city had suffered in 701 under the onslaught of Sennacherib, King of Assyria,[4] but in both 598 and 588 Nebuchadnezzar of Babylon burned and sacked Lachish. The upper picture reveals the northwest corner of the mound with some remains of the city's outer wall and several supporting buttresses. This wall was probably erected by Rehoboam about 900 B.C.[5] An inner wall was built on the crest of the mound. (The rock formation at the right was constructed by excavators.)

The middle picture shows remains of the outer gate of the double-walled city. Charring from fires that raged during the onslaught of the Babylonian army still remains on a few stones.

Just beyond the wall foundation at the right, in a debris-scattered guardroom, some twenty-one inscribed pieces of pottery were discovered. Messages had been written on them from some outpost to the commander at Lachish. One of these letters says, " . . . we are watching the signals of Lachish which my LORD is giving, for we cannot see Azekah." Perhaps Azekah had already fallen![6] Several of the letters are shown in the lower picture as they are now exhibited in the British Museum.

---

[1] Lamentations 1: 1.
[2] 2 Kings 24-25.
[3] Psalms 137.
[4] 2 Kings 18, 19.
[5] See page 33.
[6] Jeremiah 34: 7; see plate 13ab.

a. The wilderness and the Jordan Valley from above Wadi Qilt between Jerusalem and Jericho.

b. Approach to the plateau of Transjordan through the Wadi Nimrin on the road to Amman.

[Plate 20]

A Way in the Wilderness

(Wadi Qilt — Wadi Nimrin)

In the wilderness prepare the way of the Lord,
make straight in the desert a highway
for our God.
Every valley shall be lifted up,
and every mountain and hill be made low;
the uneven ground shall become level,
and the rough places a plain.
And the glory of the Lord shall be revealed, . . .[1]

h ARDLY had the smoke of battle cleared over Jerusalem when the prophet Jeremiah turned to the new task of fanning the sparks of faith that might remain in the hearts of his people. Even during the height of the siege of the city he had signed the deed to a piece of property in his home town of Anathoth[2] as a symbol of his own faith that there would be a restoration of his people.[3]

The prophet Ezekiel, taken captive in 598 with others to Babylon, related his famous "ghost story" to assure the exiles that a new day would dawn.[4] But the greatest voice of hope was one whose name has been lost, but whose writings became attached to the Book of Isaiah (chapters 34, 35, 40-66). Seen against the background of the Exile, his message is considered by many the climax of the Old Testament.

This prophet denied the existence of other gods. He called all men to faith in one supreme God, "Creator of the ends of the earth."[5] He ridiculed the idol worshipers. He gave hope to the downtrodden people — God does care! Their punishment, he told them, was but a preparation for a greater mission for God: "You are my servant, I have chosen you and not cast you off."[6] Through them all peoples of the world could be brought to Him.

Here is faith's crowning opportunity — to redeem all men. In his enthusiasm for this revelation of truth, the prophet envisaged a new world, transformed by faith. The deserts shall blossom with new life. The mountains and hills shall be leveled and the deep gorges raised to make way for the victorious Lord.

The many barren wastes in the Holy Land provide ample illustrations for these graphic words to the despairing exiles. The upper photograph, taken on the road from Jerusalem, looks east toward Jericho, across the deep Wadi Qilt.[7] Here the imagery of the prophet's words takes on vivid meaning. The words of Jesus in the parable of the Good Samaritan, "A man was going down from Jerusalem to Jericho . . .,"[8] also come forcibly to mind.

The lower view shows the rocky gorge at the approach to the plateau of Transjordan, which is also visible on the horizon in the upper picture. Oleanders grow luxuriantly along the Wadi Nimrin, lending a splash of color to the drab, rocky slopes.

---

[1] Isaiah 40: 3b-5a.
[2] See plate 12c.
[3] Jeremiah 32.
[4] Ezekiel 37.
[5] Isaiah 40: 28; 43: 10-13.
[6] Isaiah 41: 9b.
[7] Perhaps the Brook Cherith of 1 Kings 17: 3.
[8] Luke 10: 29-37.

a. *Southeast corner of the wall of Jerusalem, revealing some Herodian foundation stones.*
b. *The Citadel and David's Tower where Herod's palace once stood.*

c. *Jerusalem from the north, showing the Temple area now called the Haram esh-Sharif.*

[Plate 21]

Period of Reconstruction

(Jerusalem)

¶ *So I [Nehemiah] prayed to the God of heaven. And I said to the king [of Persia], "If it pleases the king, and if your servant has found favor in your sight, that you send me to Judah, to the city of my fathers' sepulchres, that I may rebuild it."*[1]

ALTHOUGH a few voices of encouragement were heard during those dark days of the 6th century B.C., Jerusalem still lay in ruins. The will to rebuild was not there. Faith had to be restored. Among the exiles in Babylon, however, some clung to the faith of the days of old. They awaited the day when they might return to reconstruct their devastated country.

That day came in 538 with the rise of Cyrus the Persian.[2] It was not easy, however, to arouse in people who had not known the Holy Land a vision to return. Finally in 516 B.C. the Temple was rebuilt — a far cry from the one their fathers knew, but it was a beginning. Another half century passed before the Holy City was restored. It took the energies of Haggai, Zechariah, Nehemiah, and Ezra, over a period of almost a century, to bring about even a partial reconstruction of the Holy City that Jeremiah had known.

The present city of Jerusalem is, of course, not the restored city of the 5th century B.C.; but at certain points the touch with antiquity is revealed. The upper left picture shows the southeast corner of the present Old City wall. It provides a symbol of Nehemiah's efforts to restore the wall about 440.[3] The large stones in the lower part of the present wall have remained since the time of King Herod in the early Roman period. He greatly expanded Nehemiah's wall.

The upper right picture shows part of the Citadel on the west side of the city near the present Jaffa Gate. Its present title, *David's Tower,* is misleading. Excavations within the structure have uncovered remains of Herod's huge palace. Some wall foundations may have originated in the time of the Maccabees or even Nehemiah, but nothing is there from David's time.

The lower picture views Jerusalem from the top of the tower of the beautiful new archeological museum just opposite the north wall. Here one can see how the city has spread toward the north and west (right). The building to the right of the tall single cypress tree stands today about where Nehemiah's wall joined the Temple area.

There on a high rock the Maccabees later built a fortress. Still later (c. 25 B.C.) it was expanded by Herod for his fortress Antonia.[4] There, too, begins the Via Dolorosa, meaning "Way of Sorrow," where many believe Jesus began the walk to Golgotha.[5]

---

[1] Nehemiah 2: 4b-5.
[2] Ezra 5, 6; Haggai.
[3] Nehemiah 2-4.
[4] Mark 15: 16.
[5] Mark 15: 20-22; see page 55.

a. Scrolls of the Law in the Ark of a Jewish synagogue.

b. Partial reconstruction of the synagogue at Capernaum by the Sea of Galilee.

[Plate 22]

People of the Law

(Synagogue — Capernaum)

¶ *And Ezra the priest brought the law before the assembly, both men and women and all who could hear with understanding, . . . And he read from it . . .*[1]
¶ *Blessed are those whose way is blameless, who walk in the law of the Lord!*[2]

ALTHOUGH Moses stands in biblical history as the giver of the Law,[3] Ezra is the symbol of its restoration. Among the exiles in Babylon were a few who pondered the meaning of the plight of their people. The prophets were right! The laws of the Lord had been broken. If their people would be restored to God, they must study the laws carefully and observe them faithfully. So began the study that is the heart of the Jewish faith today.

Several times before Ezra appeared[4] the people had been reminded of the law of God, beginning with Moses at Mount Sinai,[5] Joshua at Shechem,[6] and Josiah when the Law was found in the Temple.[7] Now once again, "the heads of fathers' houses of all the people, with the priests and the Levites, came together to Ezra the scribe in order to study the words of the law."[8]

The synagogue became the center for the study and teaching of the Law. By the time of Ezra it was a growing institution. It may have begun during the Exile, as those faithful to the Law gathered in homes for study and prayer. As soon as a child could learn, he was taught the Shema'[9] and the Ten Commandments,[10] the foundation of all the Law. During the centuries following Ezra, schools of interpretation of the Law began to grow, and a vast literature developed. Only those specially trained were capable of interpreting its contents. Thus scribes, priests, and later the rabbis became an important segment of Jewish society. At the heart of all their studies lay the *Torah*, the first five books of the Old Testament.

The upper picture reveals the interior of an Ark, which is the focal point of every Jewish synagogue. Within the Ark stand the sacred scrolls of the Law. They are written on parchment by skilled scribes who follow with great precision the details laid down for copying sacred documents. The scroll on the right is opened to the Book of Exodus. The Ten Commandments appear in the lower middle column indicated by generous spacing of the Hebrew words.

The lower photograph shows the partial restoration of a synagogue at Capernaum by the Sea of Galilee.[11] Though built in the 3rd century A.D., it doubtless stands on the foundation of the one in which Jesus taught, according to the Gospel records.[12]

---

[1] Nehemiah 8: 2-3a.
[2] Psalms 119: 1.
[3] *Torah*, or "divine teaching."
[4] c. 400 B.C.
[5] See page 15.
[6] See plate 2b and page 19.
[7] See page 37.
[8] Nehemiah 8: 13.
[9] Deuteronomy 6: 4.
[10] Exodus 20.
[11] See plate 24a.
[12] Mark 1: 21.

a. Bethlehem framed in the olive trees surrounding the Shepherds' Fields.

b. Looking southeast across modern Nazareth on the southern edge of the hills of Galilee.

[Plate 23]

Ḣope for the Messiah

(Bethlehem — Nazareth)

But you, O Bethlehem Ephrathah,
 who are little to be among the clans of Judah,
from you shall come forth for me
 one who is to be ruler in Israel, . . .[1]
¶ *And Joseph also went up from Galilee, from*
the city of Nazareth, to Judea, to the city of
David, which is called Bethlehem, because he
was of the house and lineage of David, . . .[2]

EVENTS in the Holy Land moved swiftly after the time of Ezra, though the biblical records are meager. Persian rule collapsed under the pressure of Alexander of Macedon in 331. His empire, in turn, broke into four parts. The Holy Land then became a pawn between the Greek forces of Egypt and Syria.

Greek culture was forced upon the Jews until the desecration of the Temple in 168 B.C.[3] fanned the flames of revolt. Then the Jews gained a brief period of independence under the Maccabees (or Hasmoneans). The rededication of the Temple in 165 B.C. is still celebrated in December, as the Feast of Hannukah,[4] one of the primary festivals of the Jewish year.

Barely a hundred years later the little country once again felt the heel of a foreign conqueror as Pompey won the Holy Land for Rome in 63 B.C.

In the meantime the writings of the prophets had achieved a place of authority beside the *Torah*. The faith of the people was strengthened by the prophetic hope that God would intervene in the turbulent world by sending one who would truly be *the anointed* — the Messiah. Many leaders arose to claim the title, for a time gained a following, but soon disappeared.[5] Then in Bethlehem a babe was born whom the world can never forget.

Bethlehem is rich in the traditions of both Jews and Christians. The "Shepherds' Fields," which appear in the foreground of the upper picture, recede toward the hills on which modern Bethlehem is spread. These are also identified as the fields of Boaz in the story of Ruth. Here, too, was the home of David. The city has spread far beyond the original humble village. The bell towers at the left rise over the Church of the Nativity on the hill, a constant scene of Christian pilgrimage.

Far to the north on the edge of the Plain of Esdraelon[6] nestles the city of Nazareth among the hills of Galilee. It, too, has grown to great size in recent centuries, as another Christian center. Here was the home that Jesus knew for many years in a humble Jewish carpenter's family. The lower view looks to the southeast across the main part of Nazareth toward Mount Gilboa[7] on the far side of the plain. On the hill of Moreh[8] in the distance at the left are Indur,[9] Nein[10] and Sulam.[11]

---

[1] Micah 5: 2.
[2] Luke 2: 4.
[3] Daniel 8: 11; 11: 31;
   1 Maccabees 1: 20-64.

[4] "Feast of Dedication."
[5] Acts 5: 36-39.
[6] See plates 13c and 18b.
[7] See plate 13c.

[8] Judges 7: 1.
[9] Endor of 1 Samuel 28.
[10] Nain of Luke 7: 11.
[11] Shunem; see page 27.

a. The Sea of Galilee from Capernaum, looking west toward the hills of Galilee.

b. The Plain of Gennesaret on the western shore of the Sea of Galilee.

[Plate 24]

Proclaiming the Good News

(SEA OF GALILEE)

¶ . . . he [Jesus] withdrew into Galilee; and leaving Nazareth he went and dwelt in Capernaum by the sea, . . . And he went about all Galilee, teaching in their synagogues and preaching the gospel of the kingdom . .[1]

ONE day a large crowd gathered at the River Jordan,[2] listening to the preaching of a rugged wilderness figure called John the Baptist. His theme was the "good news"[3] of the kingdom of heaven which he believed was soon to be ushered in. He called the people to repent and to be baptized as a confession of sins.

From among the crowd a man about thirty years of age stepped forward to be baptized. John hesitated, but under pressure he consented and baptized Jesus of Nazareth. Soon Jesus returned to Galilee, where he spent most of his brief ministry, centered at Capernaum.

From the shores of the Sea of Galilee he watched the fishermen at their work and called some to be disciples and "fishers of men."[4] In the synagogues, by the sea, from a boat, on the Plain of Gennesaret, in the surrounding hills, in the villages—wherever people would gather to hear – he taught them about the kingdom of God.

No visit to the Holy Land is complete for Christians without a walk beside the Sea of Galilee. Approaching it from Nazareth to the west, one's first glimpse of the Sea, which bursts upon him as he mounts the last high hill, brings a thrill he can never forget. There, more than a thousand feet below, etched sharply against the steep, barren cliffs to the east, lies the Sea. Like a sapphire in a setting of gold, it silently testifies to the teaching which made its shores sacred. The upper picture views the Sea of Galilee (685 feet below sea level) from Capernaum on its northern shore. Looking west to the hills of Galilee, the "Horns of Hattin," identified by some with the Sermon on the Mount,[5] rise abruptly in the center.

Just beyond the streak of shimmering sun on the lake, the fertile Plain of Gennesaret[6] slopes gently up toward the hills. In the lower picture luxuriant banana trees surround the vegetable gardens on the plain. The Sea is barely visible beyond the trees.

On the horizon the lava-strewn volcanic hills of Bashan[7] stretch out in sharp contrast to the fertile foreground. The healthy cows of Bashan provided the prophet Amos with a sarcastic metaphor when he spoke to the women of Bethel about 760 B.C.[8] In the time of Jesus, that was the area ruled by Philip.[9] To the right is the "country of the Gerasenes" in the Decapolis.[10]

---

[1] Matthew 4: 12b-13a, 23a.
[2] See plate 8a and page 17.
[3] The meaning of *gospel*.
[4] Matthew 4: 18-22.
[5] Matthew 5-7.
[6] Mark 6: 53.
[7] The land of Og in the time of Moses; Numbers 21: 33.
[8] Amos 4: 1.
[9] Luke 3: 1.
[10] Mark 5: 1, 20; see plate 29b.

a. Cluster of anemones in the garden of the Palestine Archaeological Museum in Jerusalem.

b. Looking north from the foot of Mount Gerizim toward Jacob's Well and the village of 'Askar.

[Plate 25]

ABOUT THE AUTHOR

JOHN C. TREVER is the A. J. Humphreys Professor of Religion at Morris Harvey College in Charleston, West Virginia.

Born in Milwaukee in 1915, he moved with his family to California at an early age. He received his B.A. degree from the University of Southern California, and his B.D. and Ph.D. degrees from Yale University. As a fellow of the American Schools of Oriental Research, he spent eight months during 1947-1948 in the Holy Land.

To the problems presented by this book Dr. Trever has brought an array of talent. He is, first of all, a devout man with a background of learning. He is an expert photographer with a sharp sense of composition and color. He is, moreover, a forceful writer with one eye fixed on biblical accuracy and the other on dramatic presentation.

Dr. Trever is a frequent contributor to religious journals and publications. He is well-known internationally for the part he played in the discovery of the famous "Dead Sea Scrolls," on whose publication he is still engaged.

In this book on the Holy Land, "Cradle of Our Faith," Dr. Trever's talents have culminated to produce a vivid portrait of a country deeply suffused with faith and the presence of God.

Looking west from the Mount of Olives across the Valley of the Kidron to the Old City of Jerusalem, the city of many Churches.

"O Men of Little Faith"

(LILIES OF THE FIELD — JACOB'S WELL)

¶ *"Therefore I tell you, do not be anxious about your life, . . . Consider the lilies of the field, how they grow; they neither toil nor spin; yet I tell you, even Solomon in all his glory was not arrayed like one of these."*[1]
¶ *So he came to a city of Samaria, called Sychar, near the field that Jacob gave to his son Joseph. Jacob's well was there, and so Jesus, wearied as he was with his journey, sat down beside the well.*[2]

JESUS taught in parables which gave meaning and content to life. His stories were simple, graphic, touching the human heart, giving inspiration and encouragement. His faith was contagious. Here was a man who spoke with a new authority. He taught the old Law, but it was new. Lives were changed. Hate turned to love, evil to good. The sick were made well. Minds were healed. Thus many began to see in him the Messiah[3] for whom they had longed.

Many a tourist in the Holy Land has been disappointed to discover that only a few places mentioned in the Gospels are definitely known. Most of the traditional sites can be traced no earlier than to the 4th century, when the Roman Empire adopted Christianity. Regardless of this lack, however, living symbols of the ministry of Jesus abound in the countryside — flowers, trees and animals. Many of these served to illustrate his intimate messages. Today they give life to the ancient story.

Such a cluster of anemones as is shown in the upper picture never fails to bring to mind the lesson about worry in the Sermon on the Mount. No one knows which flower Jesus meant in Matthew 6: 25, but the profusion of anemones splashed over the hillsides in the springtime makes them a likely guess. Jesus continued, "But if God so clothes the grass of the field, which today is alive and tomorrow is thrown into the oven,

will he not much more clothe you, O men of little faith?"[4]

One site clearly identified, as already indicated (plate 4bc), is Jacob's Well near ancient Shechem. It lay along the highland route which Jesus would have followed between Galilee and Jerusalem. The story of Jesus stopping at the well vividly portrays his teaching for life.[5] The lower picture views Jacob's Well from the south. The Arab village of 'Askar (Sychar?) nestles at the foot of Mount Ebal half a mile to the north.

'Askar has been thought by many to be the village from which the Samaritan woman came to draw water when she met Jesus. Recent excavations at Balata, to the left just beyond range of the picture,[6] between Mount Gerizim and Mount Ebal and closer to Jacob's Well than 'Askar, have convinced others that Balata was the site. Thus Sychem (Shechem) was probably meant by the Gospel writer, as in Acts 7: 16.

---

[1] Matthew 6: 25a; 28b-29.
[2] John 4: 5-6.
[3] In Greek, "the Christ."
[4] Matthew 6: 30.
[5] John 4.
[6] See plate 2b.

a. The Gardens of Gethsemane on the Mount of Olives, seen from the east wall of Jerusalem.

b. The Latin Garden of Gethsemane with the wall of Jerusalem framed in the old olive trees.

[Plate 26]

Agony in the Garden

(Garden of Gethsemane)

¶ *And when they had sung a hymn, they went out to the Mount of Olives. . . . And they went to a place which was called Gethsemane; and he said to his disciples, "Sit here, while I pray. . . . My soul is very sorrowful, even to death; remain here, and watch."*[1]

THE annual celebration of the Passover, the primary festival of the Jewish year,[2] attracted Jews from near and far to the Temple in Jerusalem. Thus Jesus headed toward Jerusalem one spring about A.D. 29. His arrival there touched off a series of momentous events, which have left their indelible stamp upon the world.

At first crowds greeted him, as many sought to hear him. In the Temple he taught, but provoked the Roman-inclined priests and scribes.[3] Tension mounted. Finally, with a few loyal disciples, he sought the privacy of a home in which to share a simple meal.

In that "upper room" he impressed upon them the deep meaning of his impending agony through a symbolic act of breaking bread and sharing the cup. Then, together, they left the city, crossed the Valley of the Kidron[4] to a quiet garden on the Mount of Olives. The disciples, wearied and confused by the week of stirring experiences, fell asleep, leaving Jesus to struggle alone.

Of course no one knows exactly where Jesus knelt in prayer that night, but to Christians the Mount of Olives is synonymous with deep searching of one's faith. Today monasteries have been built around old, gnarled olive trees in living memory of that agony in the garden. The upper photograph, taken from the southeast wall of the Temple area, looks east across the Valley of the Kidron, divided between colorful fruit orchards and somber graveyards, to the Mount with its Gardens of Gethsemane. At the left is the beautiful new Latin church, The Basilica of the Agony, adjacent to a Franciscan monastery surrounding some of the older olive trees on the Mount. Higher up, the Russian Orthodox Church of Saint Mary Magdalene, with its characteristic spires, projects above the trees of another walled garden called Gethsemane.

In the lower picture we view the beautifully tended Franciscan garden. Tender olive branches frame the Valley of the Kidron and the wall of the Old City of Jerusalem. The Dome, marking the Temple site, rises above the wall. Through the olive leaves to the right can be seen the now closed "Golden Gate" which was an eastern entrance to Jerusalem in the time of Jesus. In the peace of the garden, surrounded by friendly olive trees, the pilgrim today finds strength for his faith as he ponders that story of long ago.

---

[1] Mark 14: 26, 32, 34. [3] Mark 11: 15-18. [4] John 18: 1.
[2] See page 13.

a. The "Station of the Cross" in the Church of the Holy Sepulchre.

b. "Gordon's Calvary," a skull-like cliff just north of the Damascus Gate of Jerusalem.

[Plate 27]

The Path to Golgotha

(JERUSALEM — CALVARY)

¶ *And they brought him to the place called Golgotha (which means the place of a skull). . . . And they crucified him, . . .* [1]

HAVING been betrayed by one of his disciples in the Garden of Gethsemane, Jesus was captured by accomplices of the Roman-appointed High Priest, Caiaphas, and taken back to Jerusalem. His followers were scattered. Before daybreak he was tried before a hastily summoned Council composed largely of aristocratic, Roman-inclined Sadducees. He was accused of blasphemy.[2]

Early in the morning Jesus was taken to the Roman governor, Pontius Pilate. Fearful lest any disturbance might move the people to revolt, Pilate yielded to the mob, which had been aroused by partisans of the chief priests to demand crucifixion.[3] Thus he turned Jesus over to his soldiers to carry out the order according to Roman practice.

To a hill called Golgotha,[4] outside the north wall of the city, they led Jesus. Exhausted from the cruel treatment by the mob and the soldiers, he stumbled under the weight of the beam he was forced to carry. There, on a cross, he died.

Tradition since the 4th century has placed Golgotha on a high rocky hill now enshrined within the Church of the Holy Sepulchre in the Old City of Jerusalem. Today pilgrims climb narrow, winding, stone steps, lighted only by burning tapers supplied by guides, to the dimly lighted chapels of the 10th, 11th, 12th and 13th "Stations of the Cross." Here the Via Dolorosa, "Way of Sorrow," which begins at the fortress Antonia,[5] nears its end.

The upper picture shows a flashlight view of the 12th Station. Its centuries-old accumulation of gifts of veneration are mostly invisible to the visitor in the dim light. Only a small bit of native stone under the altar at the extreme right (the Latin altar of Our Lady of Sorrow) is exposed to give one a conception of its original character. Under the Greek Orthodox altar at the center, the silver-plated hole is believed to be the place where the Cross stood.

The skull-like cliff in the lower picture rises outside the present wall just beyond the Damascus Gate, and has been chosen by some as the probable site. It is known as "Gordon's Calvary" from the name of the man who popularized it. At the right of the "skull," in a deeper cut in the cliff, is the entrance to Jeremiah's Grotto, said to be the place where Jeremiah wrote his Lamentations and was buried. The Garden Tomb is at left beyond camera range.[6]

---

[1] Mark 15: 22, 24a.
[2] Mark 14: 53-65.
[3] Mark 15: 11-15.
[4] "The Skull"; in Latin, *Calvary.*
[5] See plate 21c and page 43.
[6] See plate 28b.

a. The entrance to the Chapel of the Holy Sepulchre.

b. The Garden Tomb near the foot of "Gordon's Calvary."

[Plate 28]

Victory over Death

(THE EMPTY TOMB)

¶ *When it was evening, there came a rich man from Arimathea, named Joseph, who also was a disciple of Jesus. He went to Pilate and asked for the body of Jesus. Then Pilate ordered it to be given to him. And Joseph took the body, and wrapped it in a clean linen shroud, and laid it in his own new tomb, . . .*[1]

TOWARD evening of that ill-fated day with the Sabbath approaching, hasty preparations were made to place the body of Jesus in a nearby tomb, offered by Joseph of Arimathea. Early on the morning following the Sabbath, some of the women who had kept vigil at the cross went to the tomb with preparations for a more suitable burial. The tomb was empty! He had triumphed over death!

The Cross was not the end. "He is risen!" became a mighty chorus of the reawakened faith of his many followers. It has echoed down the centuries from the voices of those who have found victory through his living presence.

Jeremiah had promised a new covenant of the Law written on human hearts;[2] Ezekiel had preached about a new heart;[3] in Jesus many found, through faith, the living reality of all the Old Testament promises.

The tradition for the location of the tomb of Jesus can be traced with certainty only to the 4th century, when the mother of Constantine sought to identify the holy places. For the pilgrim today, it is difficult to imagine an ancient tomb cut from the native rock in the chapel (the 14th Station) beneath the huge rotunda of the Church of the Holy Sepulchre.

The upper picture shows the tomb completely surrounded by the marble chapel reconstructed in 1810. Just inside the entrance, beside which stand a Greek Orthodox monk (left) and a Franciscan friar (right), is the Angel's Chapel. In the center, encased in marble, stands a stone believed to be the one used to close the entrance to the tomb. Beyond is the low entrance to the small Chapel of the Holy Sepulchre, on the right side of which sits a marble altar said to cover the original tomb.

Excavations in the late 19th century at the foot of the cliff to the left of Gordon's Calvary[4] uncovered a large tomb cut out of solid rock. Nearby were evidences of an early Christian church, which led some to believe that here might have been the original tomb. Around this tomb has been developed a lovely garden (lower picture) with many native plants and trees of the Bible. Though the study of early tombs has made the identification of this site very doubtful, many pilgrims find that here in the Garden Tomb the resurrection story becomes a living experience. It is certainly one of the most beautiful spots in Jerusalem.

---

[1] Matthew 27: 57-60a.
[2] Jeremiah 31: 31-34.
[3] Ezekiel 36: 26, 27.
[4] See plate 27b.

a. Some of the remains of the ancient harbor built by King Herod at Caesarea.

b. Looking southeast across modern Tiberias on the western shore of the Sea of Galilee.

[Plate 29]

A.D. 30 – C. 330

The Struggle with Paganism

(CAESAREA – TIBERIAS)

¶ *On the morrow we departed and came to Caesarea; and we entered the house of Philip the evangelist, who was one of the seven, and stayed with him.*[1] ¶ *Some were tortured, ... Others suffered mocking, scourging, and even chains and imprisonment. They were stoned ... they were killed with the sword; ...*[2]

THE new faith in God through Christ spread rapidly in the Holy Land and, under the dynamic preaching of Peter and Paul, soon left the "Cradle" to permeate the whole Roman Empire.[3] Meanwhile Judaism continued to propagate its faith in God through Moses and the *Torah*. At first hostile toward one another, the two faiths soon recognized a common foe in Roman paganism.

With paganism there could be no compromise for either Jew or Christian. Rome ruled over both, but both outlived Rome. Both faced devastating persecutions late in the 1st century. Jerusalem fell to Titus in A.D. 70. At the end of the century the Christians suffered terribly under Domitian.

In 132 the Jews revolted under Bar Kochba but were crushed by Hadrian in 135. Then for almost two centuries Jerusalem remained a pagan city, called *Aelia Capitolina*. A few small Christian groups continued in the Holy Land, mainly at Caesarea and Pella.[4] Some Jewish settlements developed at Jamnia,[5] Sepphoris,[6] and Tiberias.

The upper picture, taken at Caesarea, shows some remains of Herod's breakwater and harbor still lying along the shore of the Mediterranean at the upper end of the Plain of Sharon.[7] First built in 13 B.C., Caesarea became the seat of the Roman government under the procurators. Peter visited Cornelius there,[8] and later Paul visited Philip the evangelist.[9] About A.D. 60 Paul was imprisoned there for two years by Felix the governor.[10] In the 3rd century Origen and Pamphilus developed their great library of sacred writings at Caesarea, and Eusebius about A.D. 330 prepared fifty vellum manuscripts of the Greek Bible for the Roman Emperor Constantine. The Christians of Caesarea suffered horrible persecutions under Diocletian about 300.

Tiberias (lower photograph), on the western shore of the Sea of Galilee, was developed by Herod Antipas, Tetrarch of Galilee and Perea.[11] In the 2nd century Tiberias became the chief center of learning for the Jews and the headquarters for the Sanhedrin. There the Mishnah, the basic code of interpretation of the Law, was compiled about 200, and later the Jerusalem Talmud.

The blue Sea of Galilee stretches off toward the south, with the hills of the region of the Decapolis beyond.[12]

---

[1] Acts 21: 8.
[2] Hebrews 11: 35-37.
[3] Book of Acts.
[4] In the upper Jordan Valley.
[5] South of Jaffa.
[6] In central Galilee.
[7] See plate 31a.
[8] Acts 10: 1-23.
[9] Acts 21: 8-16.
[10] Acts 23: 23–24: 27.
[11] 4 B.C. – A.D. 39.
[12] See plate 24b.

a. The Dome of the Rock from the northwest, symbolic of Jewish, Christian, and Muslim Faith.

b. Detail view of the lower ceiling of the Dome with its abstract geometric art.
c. Details of a cornice extending from a supporting marble pillar under the Dome.

[Plate 30]

Unity in Faith

(Jerusalem – Dome of the Rock)

*. . . they who wait for the LORD shall
renew their strength,
they shall mount up with wings like eagles,
they shall run and not be weary,
they shall walk and not faint.*[1]
¶ *We know that in everything God works for
good with those who love him, who are called
according to his purpose.*[2] ¶ *We believe in
that which hath been revealed unto us and
revealed unto you; our God and your God is
One, and unto Him we surrender.*[3]

AS we have followed the story of faith in the Holy Land, we have seen it wax and wane through many vicissitudes of history. We must now jump ahead three centuries after the recognition of Christianity by the Roman Empire,[4] to the emergence of a new expression of faith – Islam, the religion of Mohammedans.

In 637 the Muslims, as they are commonly called, moved out from Arabia, where Mecca and Medina had become their most holy places, to gain control of the Holy Land along with most of the Middle East.

With the roots of their Islamic faith penetrating deeply into the Judeo-Christian past, they too considered many sites in the Holy Land sacred. Jerusalem became their third most sacred city.[5] Many believed that the prophet Mohammed ascended to heaven from the rock on which Solomon's Temple once stood. There the Caliph 'Abd el-Malik erected in 691 the beautiful Dome of the Rock, the Muslims' most sacred place in the Holy Land.[6]

The Dome of the Rock, therefore, stands today as a symbol of a basic unity in faith. Its combination of Byzantine-Christian and Arabic art, developed by Muslims on a site that is sacred also to Jews, carries a meaning that transcends time and space. In this abstract, geometric art one's imagination is carried away in reverent contemplation of that which is spiritual. Here is a fitting symbol of faith which has drawn man toward God as he has sought strength for daily tasks and the understanding of, and meaning for, life. Whether a prayer be uttered by Jew, Christian or Muslim, it is the soul's sincere desire expressed in faith to One who is the Father of all.

In the upper photograph appears the octagonal-shaped Dome of the Rock. The sun glistens on its dome as though a reflection of Divine Providence radiating His love upon all men who seek Him in faith. As one enters the memorial building, the breath-taking beauty of the abstract art of the ceiling (lower left) and the intricate details of the cornices (lower right) on the supporting pillars speak of the universality of faith. One is moved to utter a prayer of thanksgiving to God, the Creator of all that is beautiful and good.

---

[1] Isaiah 40: 31.
[2] Romans 8: 28.
[3] The Koran, Surah 29: 46b.
[4] A.D. 311.
[5] Arabs still call it *El Quds*, "The Holy Place."
[6] See *Frontispiece* and plates one and 15c.

a. Air view of the Plain of Sharon ten miles north of Caesarea, near Mount Carmel.

b. The 2000-year-old scroll of Isaiah from a cave by the Dead Sea, showing Isaiah 38: 9—40: 28.

[Plate 31]

Peoples of the Book

(PLAIN OF SHARON — DEAD SEA SCROLL)

" . . . so shall my word be that goes forth
from my mouth;
it shall not return to me empty,
but it shall accomplish that which I purpose,
and prosper in the thing for which I sent it."[1]
¶ *All scripture is inspired by God and profitable*
for teaching, for reproof, for correction, and for
training in righteousness, that the man of God
may be complete, equipped for every good work.[2]
¶ *Is it not enough for them that We have sent*
down unto thee the Scripture which is read unto
them? Lo! herein verily is mercy, and a reminder
for folk who believe.[3]

AS we have turned the pages of history to discover the story of faith, we have caught glimpses of almost every part of the Holy Land. Now, as we leave that fascinating land of antiquity, let us take a last look at one section which our visits have failed to include — the Plain of Sharon, extolled by poets for its beauty.[4]

There below (upper picture) is the fertile plain, a patchwork of luxuriant fields promising abundant crops for hungry people. Here, about ten miles north of Caesarea,[5] the plain narrows as the Mount Carmel range presses it out toward the sea and separates the Plain of Esdraelon from the coast. We have just passed Tantura.[6]

At the right is the modern village of Kafr Lam, and nestled in the foothills of Mount Carmel just above the center is 'Ein Ghazal. Far in the distance we catch a last glimpse of Mount Gilboa.[7] To the left Mount Carmel soon reaches its highest point not far from where Elijah held his contest with the priests of Baal.[8]

As the scenes from this great stage of history on which the story of faith was enacted have been viewed, one is mindful that the messages out of the living past have been preserved through the writings which the actors left behind. Those who enacted these scenes in life became "Peoples of the Book" — the Old Testament, the New Testament, or the Koran. Had it not been for that fact, these places might not have retained their sacred associations in the minds of later generations.

Had not the ancients seen God at work in that drama of history and been convinced that He had spoken through the recorded word, man today would be spiritually poorer indeed. Thus the story which has been reviewed here in pictures and brief commentary is but an invitation to go to the Scriptures to study further the message of faith.

A fitting symbol of all Scriptures from antiquity is the famed Isaiah Scroll, recently found in a cave by the Dead Sea. The lower picture shows this scroll which is the oldest biblical document yet discovered.[9]

---

[1] Isaiah 55: 11.
[2] 2 Timothy 3: 16-17.
[3] The Koran, Surah 29: 51.
[4] Isaiah 35: 2.
[5] See plate 29a.
[6] Ancient Dor, Judges 1: 27.
[7] See plate 13c.
[8] 1 Kings 18: 20-40.
[9] See plate 32.

The opening columns of the Dead Sea Scroll of Isaiah, showing chapters 1: 1–5: 14 (reading from right to left).

[Plate 32]

Epilogue

All flesh is grass,
and all its beauty is like the flower
of the field . . .
The grass withers, the flower fades;
but the word of our God will stand forever.[1]

IN the spring of 1947 a group of Bedouins, traveling along the northwestern shore of the Dead Sea,[2] happened upon a cave high up on a nearby cliff.[3] In this cave they found some large, early Roman type jars, each with an earthenware bowl cover. Some contained rolls of old leather manuscripts wrapped in linen cloth.

They took the scrolls to Bethlehem[4] and there consulted a friend, a Syrian Orthodox Christian merchant. With his help they sold four of the scrolls to the Saint Mark's Syrian Orthodox Monastery in the Old City of Jerusalem. Several months later the Bedouins sold three other scrolls to the Hebrew University in Jerusalem.

Two of the manuscripts proved to be scrolls of Isaiah in ancient Hebrew script, one dating from the early 1st century B.C. and the other from the early 1st century A.D. The older of the two, the Saint Mark's Scroll, contains the entire book of Isaiah except for a few small breaks. Twenty-four feet long by ten inches wide, this scroll was prepared by sewing together seventeen sheets of sheepskin. It was copied over a thousand years before the otherwise oldest existing Hebrew manuscript of Isaiah, and is now the earliest known biblical document.

Since this important discovery was made, a flood of manuscript fragments has come from other caves in this same region by the Dead Sea, where apparently a group of Essenes (an ancient Jewish sect) lived and studied their sacred Scriptures. The remains of their community center have been uncovered at Khirbet Qumran near the caves, of which six have yielded manuscript fragments. These startling discoveries have awakened in many people a new enthusiasm for research and study of ancient Scriptures.

Plate 31b shows the beautifully preserved Saint Mark's Isaiah Scroll opened to chapter 40, where the Hebrew words quoted in translation above from Isaiah appear seven lines down in the middle

---

[1] Isaiah 40: 6b, 8.   [3] See plate 8b.   [4] See plate 23a.
[2] See plate 8c.

column. We are reminded that what God has written on the hearts of men is eternal. Whether it be words from the Old Testament of Jews, the New Testament of Christians, or the Koran of Muslims, that which inspires men to deeper faith and nobler living is of God.

It has been our prayer that this quest might bring to a focus that faith which forms the warp and woof of the Word of God, and thereby provide a bond of unity that could draw all men into closer fellowship, brotherhood and peace. The final photograph, therefore, presents again the ancient Saint Mark's Scroll of Isaiah opened this time to the first four columns. In the second column from the right (lines 11-13; Isaiah 2: 4) appear in early Hebrew script those words of hope which lend a fitting benediction to our quest:

> *He shall judge between the nations,*
> *and shall decide for many peoples;*
> *and they shall beat their swords into plowshares,*
> *and their spears into pruning hooks;*
> *nation shall not lift up sword against nation,*
> *neither shall they learn war any more.*

Supplements

EARLY CHRONOLOGY OF THE HOLY LAND

GLOSSARY OF UNUSUAL WORDS

SUGGESTIONS FOR FURTHER READING

MAP LOCATING PHOTOGRAPHS

ACKNOWLEDGEMENTS

Early Chronology of the Holy Land

Biblical and Post-biblical Periods		Archeological Periods	
Patriarchs (Abraham, etc.)	c. 2000—c. 1700 B.C.	Middle Bronze Age	2100—1600 B.C.
Egyptian Sojourn and Bondage	c. 1700—c. 1280	Late Bronze Age	1600—1200
Exodus and Wilderness Wanderings	c. 1280—c. 1240		
Conquest and Judges	c. 1240—c. 1020	Iron I (Early)	1200—900
United Kingdom	c. 1020—c. 925		
Divided Kingdom	c. 925—587	Iron II (Middle)	900—587
Writing Prophets	760 and following		
Dispersion of the Northern tribes	722/1		
Conquest of Judah	587	Iron III (Late)	587—333
Babylonian Exile	587—538		
Reconstruction	520—331	Persian	
Greek Period	331—168	Hellenistic	333—63
Maccabean Independence	165—63		
Roman Conquest and Rule	63 B.C.—A.D. 325	Roman	63 B.C.—A.D. 325
Herod the Great	37—4 B.C.		
Procurators	A.D. 6—42		
Fall of Jerusalem	70		
Revolt of Bar Kochba	132		
Pagan rule	135—c. 325		
Christian domination	c. 325—637	Byzantine	325—637
Muslim control	637 and following	Arab	637 and following

Glossary of Unusual Words

AMORITE—The common name given to the people who inhabited the Holy Land prior to the entrance of the Hebrews under Joshua. Their name came from the Babylonian word, *Amurru*, meaning "the west country," which applied to the area north and west of Babylon (northeast of Palestine) where the Amorites (or, *Amurrites*) first settled. Mari (modern Tell Hariri), recently excavated on the middle Euphrates River, was their chief center. In the Bible Amorite and Canaanite often refer to the same people. Sometimes the term Canaanite refers more specifically to the pre-Hebrew inhabitants of the coastlands and valleys, while the term Amorite then refers to those who lived in the highlands.

ARCHEOLOGY—The systematic study of ancient remains of civilization for the purpose of supplementing and clarifying the known literary records. This field of study has been particularly revealing for students of the Bible. Scientific archeology began in the Holy Land in 1890 with the brief but exacting excavation conducted at Tell el-Hesi (probably the city of Eglon mentioned in the Bible) by Sir Flinders Petrie, the famed British archeologist. He systematically recorded and photographed every object and type of pottery found in each level uncovered in the mound. Thus he laid a foundation for comparison of similar levels in any other mound excavated in that country. See page 33 and plate 16b.

ARK OF THE COVENANT—According to Exodus 25:10-22, the Ark was an oblong box made of acacia wood (in Hebrew, *shittim*), probably the *Acacia seyal* very common in Sinai. It was covered with gold and topped with two golden cherubim whose outstretched wings surrounded the "Mercy Seat" which indicated the presence of God. The Ark contained the two tables of the Law by which the covenant between God and Israel had been established. Carried by long poles inserted in golden rings on each corner, the Ark led the way during the wilderness wanderings under Moses. See page 21.

BAALISM—The religion of the Canaanites. It included the worship of many gods, idols, and fertility elements, all of which were foreign to the Hebrews who worshiped the one God, YHWH (see LORD). The most prominent god of the Canaanites was Baal, the storm and fertility god, from whom the designation arose.

BEDOUIN—An Arabic term referring to one who dwells in the desert. He lives in tents, usually made of goat's hair, and he moves about as the needs of his flocks demand. The more general term, nomad, refers to the same kind of person.

BIRKET—The Arabic word for "pool." For instance, Birket es-Sultan means literally, "The Pool of the Sultan." It is a large depression (perhaps once a reservoir) on the southwest side of Jerusalem and forms the upper end of the Valley of Hinnom (see plate 14).

CANAANITE—See Amorite.

DECAPOLIS—A league of ten Greek cities, mostly in Transjordan. The name is Greek, meaning literally, "ten-cities." They occupied a region extending from Damascus to modern Amman (biblical Rabbah, called by the Greeks, Philadelphia). The main group of these thoroughly Hellenized cities was located south and east of the Sea of Galilee and more specifically referred to as "the region of the Decapolis" (Mark 7: 31). A portion of the region extended west of the Jordan to include Beth-shan (modern Beisan), called by the Greeks Scythopolis. The best known of the cities of the Decapolis today is Jerash (ancient Gerasa) whose remains have been uncovered and much of the city restored to the delight of every visitor to the Kingdom of the Jordan.

'EIN (also spelled 'ain) — The Arabic word for a spring of fresh water. The plural form is 'ayun, as in 'Ayun Musa, "Springs of Moses."

ESSENES—A devoutly religious sect of Jews which apparently originated during the second century B. C. They were extremely conservative, living apart in a semi-monastic type of community. They were very devoted to the study of the Scriptures, many copies of which are just now being discovered near what was evidently their community center at Khirbet Qumran by the Dead Sea. There are some indications which suggest that John the Baptist, and perhaps even Jesus, might have belonged to this sect for a time.

HARAM—The Arabic word which designates a sanctuary or sacred place, like the Haram esh-Sharif, "the Noble Sanctuary" (page 31). In this case the name designates the enclosed sacred area in which the Dome of the Rock and the Mosque el Aksa now stand.

HYKSOS—An Egyptian term which applies to the Semitic peoples who invaded Egypt toward the end of the 18th century B.C. They were a mixed group of northwest Semites, mostly from Syria and Palestine. Some non-Semitic peoples seem also to have been included. They introduced the horse and chariot into warfare and built huge rectangular, thick-walled fortifications. They were finally driven out of Egypt about 1570 by Ahmose I. The empire of the Hyksos was ruled from Zoan (also called Avaris, Tanis, and later Rameses) in the northeastern Delta of the Nile. See page 11.

ISLAM—An Arabic word which refers to the religion of the followers of Mohammed. It means "submission." Those who submit to the will of 'Allah (Arabic for "God") as taught by Mohammed and his followers belong to the faith of Islam. This is the faith of most of the peoples of the Middle East.

KHIRBET—An Arabic term meaning a ruin or the remains of an ancient village or fortification. The ruins are partly visible, thus distinguishing them from a tell.

LORD—Represents the sacred Name of God. The Name has been so sacred to Jews that the Hebrew word for "Lord," Adonai, has long been substituted whenever spoken. LORD is thus capitalized to indicate its distinctive usage. The pronunciation of the sacred Name, YHWH, is not definitely known. The story of the revelation of the sacred Name to Moses is found in Exodus 3: 13-15.

MACCABEAN TIMES—The period of Jewish history from 165 B.C. to 63 B.C. The name originated from Judas Maccabeus (literally, Judas, "the Hammerer") and his brothers who led the revolt against the Greek overlord, Antiochus Epiphanes. Antiochus had tried to force Greek culture on the Jews, and in 168 B.C. desecrated the Temple in Jerusalem by offering swine's flesh as a sacrifice. This period of political independence is also known as the Hasmonean period from the family name of Judas and the other rulers and leaders. See pages 19, 43 and 47.

MIDDLE EAST—That area of the world which includes modern Turkey, Syria, Jordan, Israel, Egypt, Saudi Arabia, Iraq, Iran and some other adjacent countries. The term "Near East" is also frequently used for this area.

MINARET—A tall, slender tower topped with a covered platform. One is associated with every Muslim mosque. The muezzin calls the faithful Muslims to prayer several times each day from this tower.

MOSQUE—The place for private and group worship for Muslims. It is equivalent to the synagogue of the Jews and the church of the Christians. On Friday, the Muslim holy day, special services are conducted in the mosque. Since every Muslim worshiper must face toward Mecca (the capital of Arabia and the Muslims' most holy place) when he prays, a niche, called the *mihrab,* is the focal point of each mosque. It directs the worshiper toward Mecca.

MUEZZIN—The priest of a Muslim mosque who calls the faithful to prayer from the minaret.

MUSLIM (also spelled Moslem)—A follower of the prophet Mohammed (thus also called a Mohammedan). He is one who adheres to the faith of Islam. Derived from the same Arabic root as Islam ("to submit"), Muslim means literally, "one who submits," that is, to the will of *'Allah* (God).

NEGEB—A Hebrew word literally meaning "south." It refers to the barren, desert region south of Beersheba and southwest of the Dead Sea.

NOMAD—See Bedouin.

PASSOVER—The sacred festival of the Jews which commemorates the escape of their ancestors from Egypt under Moses. It originated particularly from the fact that the angel of death "passed over" the Israelite homes during the final plague in Egypt (Exodus 11, 12).

PATRIARCH—The father and leader of a family or tribe. The term applies particularly to the biblical characters, Abraham, Isaac, Jacob and his twelve sons who lived in the land of Canaan some time before 1700 B.C. They were semi-nomads who traveled about occasionally but also engaged in agriculture and established communities. See pages 5, 7 and 11.

PROCURATORS—Military officers who governed Judah (c. A.D. 6 — 42) shortly after the death of Herod the Great. They were directly responsible to the Imperial throne in Rome. Pontius Pilate is the best known of the procurators, because of his part in the trial of Jesus.

SAMARITAN—Particularly refers to one who lived in the region of Samaria after its fall to king Sargon of Assyria in 722 B.C. The Samaritans were a mixed race as a result of Assyria's deportation policy. When Samaria fell, many of her people were deported, and Sargon peopled the area with strangers to the Hebrew faith (2 Kings 17: 21-41). Gradually they adopted the Hebrew faith, but they were not welcomed into the post-Exilic Jewish community. About three hundred of them live in Nablus today.

SEMITES—A race of people said to have descended from Shem, a son of Noah (Genesis 10: 21-31). More specifically they are the people who are related to the Assyrians, Babylonians, Hebrews (later, Jews), Arabs, and others with similar Middle Eastern origins.

SHEPHELAH—A Hebrew name literally meaning "lowlands." It refers to the foothills between the Philistine plain and the southern (or Judean) highland country of Palestine.

SIROCCO (called *chamsin* by Arabs)—A hot, dry wind which blows occasionally from the Arabian desert east and southeast of the Holy Land. The dust-laden, dry air scorches everything. It creates much discomfort and often fever. In Hebrew it is an "east wind" *(qadim)*, as in Genesis 41: 6 and Hosea 13: 15. See also Luke 12: 55.

SYNAGOGUE—A Jewish place of worship and study. The focal point of the synagogue is the Ark in which the sacred scrolls of the *Torah* are kept. Services are held in the synagogue particularly on the Sabbath, which runs from sundown Friday to sundown Saturday.

TELL—The Arabic designation of a mound of accumulated debris from an ancient city. Over many centuries cities would be destroyed and rebuilt perhaps several times. Each successive layer developed because the destroyed city would be levelled and a new one built above it. At Megiddo, for instance, twenty successive layers were found, reaching a total thickness of almost seventy feet. See plate 18b.

TEREBINTH—A large-sized tree *(Pistacia terebinthus)* common to the Holy Land. It was frequently adopted by the Canaanites and the Hebrews for a sacred site (Hosea 4: 13) and is similarly used even today by the Arabs. Its Hebrew name, *'elah,* is similar to the name of the evergreen oak, *'allon,* with which it is often confused. From a distance the oak and terebinth look similar during much of the year. Unlike the oak, however, the terebinth is deciduous, losing its leaves during the winter season. (See Isaiah 6: 13 and Hosea 4: 13 where both trees are mentioned together.)

TORAH—A Hebrew term referring specifically to the first five books of the Old Testament, and more generally to all the sacred teachings of the Jews. It is often translated with the word "Law," but to the Jews today it more correctly means "Divine teaching."

WADI (also spelled *wady*)—An Arabic word referring to a valley or ravine with a stream bed. It is usually dry, except during the rainy season when it may flow with a heavy torrent.

WELI—An Arabic word referring to a holy place that is usually associated with some Muslim saint or venerated *sheikh.* Welis are seen frequently in the Holy Land on top of a hill or near a clump of oak trees or under a spreading terebinth. Archeologists have occasionally found it difficult to excavate an important ancient site where a *weli* already occupies the *tell.* Tell es-Safi is an example (see pages 5, 9 and 21).

Suggestions for Further Reading

I. Recent English Translations of Sacred Scriptures:

FOR JEWS: *The Holy Scriptures, A New Translation.* The Jewish Publication Society of America, Philadelphia, 1917.

FOR CATHOLICS: *New Catholic Edition of the Holy Bible.* Catholic Book Publishing Company, New York, 1953.

FOR MUSLIMS: *The Meaning of the Glorious Koran,* an Explanatory Translation by M. M. Pickthall. George Allen and Unwin Ltd., London, 1953. (In America: Mentor Books, The New American Library of World Literature, Inc., New York.)

FOR PROTESTANTS: *The Revised Standard Version of the Bible.* Thomas Nelson and Sons, New York, 1952.

(The author of this book has published a pamphlet entitled, "A Fresh Approach to Bible Reading," which gives a suggested outline for reading the Bible according to a historical sequence. It is available from the National Council of Churches, 79 E. Adams, Chicago 3, Illinois; three cents each, $1.50 per 100.)

II. Some Valuable Descriptive Resources Concerning the Holy Land:

W. F. ALBRIGHT, *The Archaeology of Palestine.* Penguin Books, Harmondsworth, Middlesex, England, 1954.

MILLAR BURROWS, *What Mean These Stones?* American Schools of Oriental Research, New Haven, Connecticut, 1941.

JACK FINEGAN, *Light from the Ancient Past.* Princeton University Press, Princeton, New Jersey, 1946.

NELSON GLUECK, *The River Jordan.* The Westminster Press, Philadelphia, Pennsylvania, 1946.

G. E. WRIGHT and F. V. FILSON, *The Westminster Historical Atlas to the Bible.* The Westminster Press, Philadelphia, Pennsylvania, 1945.

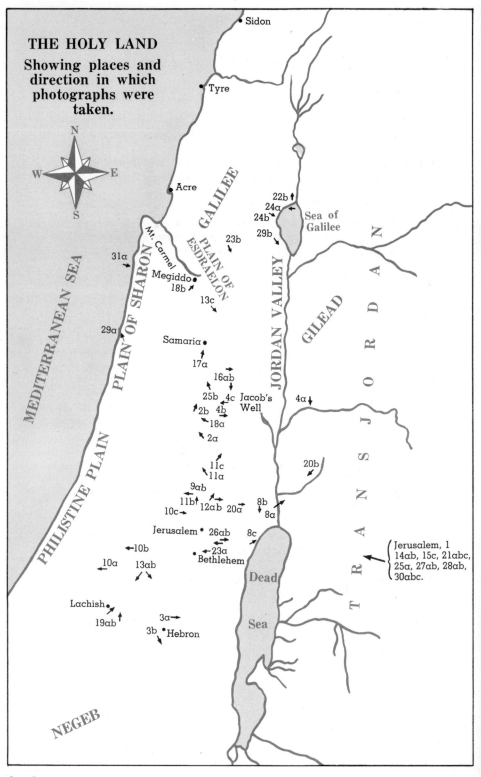

THE HOLY LAND

Showing places and direction in which photographs were taken.

N
W E
S

Sidon

Tyre

Acre

GALILEE

MEDITERRANEAN SEA

Mt. Carmel

31a

Megiddo
18b

PLAIN OF ESDRAELON

23b

22b
24a
24b
29b

Sea of Galilee

GILEAD

JORDAN VALLEY

29a

PLAIN OF SHARON

13c

Samaria

17a

16ab

25b 4c Jacob's
2b 4b Well

18a

2a

4a

11c
11a

9ab

11b

10c 12ab 20a

10b

Jerusalem 26ab

23a
Bethlehem

8c

20b

8b
8a

Dead

Sea

J O R D A N

T R A N S J O R D A N

Jerusalem, 1
14ab, 15c, 21abc,
25a, 27ab, 28ab,
30abc.

PHILISTINE PLAIN

10a 13ab

Lachish
19ab

3a
3b Hebron

NEGEB

Acknowledgements

BIBLE QUOTATIONS are from *The Revised Standard Version of the Bible,* copyrighted 1952 by the Division of Christian Education of the National Council of Churches, and used by permission.

QUOTATIONS FROM THE KORAN are from *The Meaning of the Glorious Koran,* by Mohammed Marmaduke Pickthall, published by George Allen and Unwin Ltd., London, 1953, and used with permission.

PHOTOGRAPHS unless otherwise indicated were prepared by the author with the assistance of the Board of Education of the Methodist Church, Department of Visual Education and are reproduced with permission.

PHOTOGRAPHS numbered 13c, 18b, 23b, 29a, and 29b were specially prepared by the Orient Press Photo Company, Tel Aviv, Israel.

PHOTOGRAPHS numbered 24a, 25a, 26a, and 26b, previously released for publication, are included herewith through the courtesy of John Rudin & Co., Inc., Chicago, Illinois, publishers of *The Book of Life.*

PHOTOGRAPH numbered 7 was supplied by Mr. William B. Terry and is published with his permission.

PHOTOGRAPH numbered 17c is published with the permission of the Palestine Archaeological Museum, Jerusalem.

PHOTOGRAPH numbered 19c is published with the permission of the Trustees of the late Sir Henry S. Wellcome.

THE FRONTISPIECE and photographs numbered 15c, 30a, 30b, and 30c were prepared with the assistance of the Muslim Supreme Council, Jerusalem.

PHOTOGRAPHS numbered 31b and 32 were taken with the permission of St. Mark's Syrian Orthodox Monastery, Jerusalem.

THE AUTHOR is indebted to the Ansco Company for its cooperation and counsel in the preparation of the color pictures.

Indices

INDEX OF SCRIPTURE REFERENCES

INDEX OF HISTORIC PERSONS

INDEX OF PLACE NAMES

Index of Scripture References

THE OLD TESTAMENT

Index of Historic Persons

Index of Place Names

(Lettered numbers indicate plates and photographs. Numbers without letters refer to text.)

Postscript

In keeping with the spirit and purpose of this volume, Historic Counselors, Inc. intends to develop within the near future another book following a similar plan and setting forth the story of faith among the great religions of the Far East.

[NOTES]

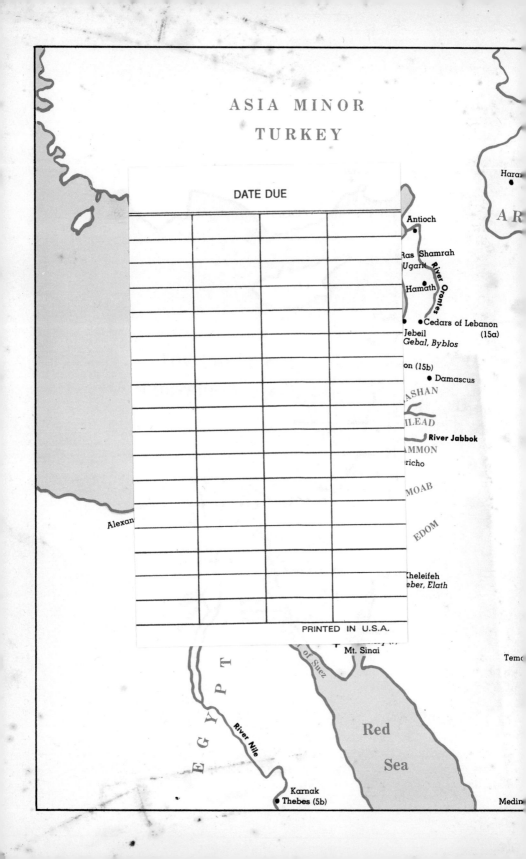

ASIA MINOR
TURKEY

DATE DUE

PRINTED IN U.S.A.